Career Path of Abundance

Career Path of Abundance

CAREER WISDOM FOR IDEALISTS SEEKING
HAPPINESS AND SUCCESS

Daryl Capuano

ISBN13: 9780984945115
ISBN: 0984945113
Learning Consultants Publishing
Library of Congress Control Number: 2015904302
The Learning Consultants, Old Saybrook, CT

To Danny, Kearney,
and Katie
Each of you is a gift

And most of all Francie
For Ensuring Happiness

Table of Contents

Introduction

Are you blessed and cursed with the wiring of an idealist? Idealists desire meaningful, purposeful, and fulfilling work. They want to make a difference, do something that matters, and make the world a better place. They view work as an extension of their identity and seek out careers that contribute to something larger than themselves. Idealists expect their work life to be a happy one.

Did you think the above statements are naïve or even foolish? If so, you are an unequivocal realist. No need to argue. Other books are more suitable for you.

The blessing of the idealist emerges from ancient wisdom: seek and ye shall find. Those who pursue happy work stand a better chance of getting it than those who are resigned to view work as a grim necessity. Given sound practical reasons, realists can accept discontent.

The curse of the idealist comes from the struggle that all seekers face when searching for the grail: the harsh reality of the nonideal world must be confronted. Here, realists often fare better because they do not suffer as much disappointment. Lower expectations are a pretty good defense mechanism.

Most people fall somewhere in the broad middle on the idealist-realist continuum, likely leaning toward one side by nature and sometimes pulled one way by circumstance. Being an idealist is a lot easier when young and single!

Idealists face a tough road. Paying the bills through work at the widget company appears a lot easier than creating a fulfilling career path with hope but no guarantee of success. Many wonder if they have to give up conventional success, most notably money and security, for a lottery chance at happy work, thinking such dreamy aspirations will lead to financial ruin and career instability.

In the last century, the "success for happiness trade off" was routinely made and, owing to economic reality, was sensible. The realistic twentieth-century Organization Man expected rock-solid security and upward mobility, but the twenty-first century has shattered those secure and mobile notions. Instead, the meteoric rise of the entrepreneur (the definition extending beyond simply launching a business to all those who actively create their work lives) happily suggests that forging an idealistic path, armed with career-building wisdom, will yield the best chance for both happiness and success.

Wisdom. That word alone should make many others put this book down. Those seeking a quick fix, a how-to manual, or three easy steps should find other helpful resources. Developing wisdom takes time. But once you have it, wisdom's everlasting quality will keep you on track for happiness and success throughout your life.

For those who wish to continue...

How to Get on the Path of Abundance

You will start with gratitude. You will reflect on how fortunate we are to be in a position to ponder career choice. Most people who have walked the earth would find such choice an extraordinary luxury. With that positive energy, you will get ready to build your career wisdom, specifically your Intrapersonal Wisdom and Entrepreneurial Wisdom.

Intrapersonal Wisdom is your inner guide. It is the wisdom that helps you understand yourself. Phrases such as "self-awareness," "emotional intelligence," and "psychological health" convey some aspects of this trait. Developing your Intrapersonal Wisdom will lead you toward work that will make you happy.

Since we choose our career paths, you might think that finding happy work is easy. You may reconsider when you think about how many people have willingly chosen work that has made them miserable. We'll define career happiness as feelings of enjoyment, satisfaction, and meaning/ purpose emanating from the work itself. Picture a master craftsman engaged in his work.

Entrepreneurial Wisdom is your outer guide. The term "entrepreneurial" is meant far more broadly than its usual business-starting definition. Phrases such as "street smarts," "political savvy," and "business sense" convey some aspects of this trait. Here, Entrepreneurial Wisdom encompasses your full practical understanding of how you will create your career. This wisdom will guide you to career success, defined here as what you derive from your work, most notably money, freedom, and self-esteem. Picture a master craftsman earning money and accolades for her work.

You will get ready to launch your career or new career path by understanding the New World of Work. Terms such as "knowledge economy," "information age," and "Internet revolution" capture parts of our current macroeconomic transformation. Most people know that the work world is changing, but few realize that the changes are as significant in scale as the Industrial Revolution. Those stuck in the mind-set of the Old World of Work—go to college, choose a secure career path, and stay employed in one organization for a few decades—need a massive operating system update.

Much like you need a more nuanced understanding of the work world, you will need to better understand yourself. To do so, you will develop key insights into your personality preferences, core motivations, and values that provide the foundation for Intrapersonal Wisdom. Developing such insight through reading, reflection, and discussions with wise friends is time consuming but necessary. Proper application and understanding of personality theory will provide a shortcut to developing Intrapersonal Wisdom.

Your drive to create a Path of Abundance—your path to both happiness and success—will be motivated in part by understanding that most people will be on either the Path of Struggle or Path of Disaster. The New World of Work will be brilliant for the few, tough for many, and brutal for some.

You will then dig more deeply into your idiosyncratic understanding of happiness and success. Why? Because most people have only a vague notion of what each means to them. Your happiness and success criteria will be unique to your vision.

From there, you will then get set to launch your career by understanding how different types of work will lead to your Path of Abundance. If you are currently working in a job that you detest, or have to take a job that is not part of your long-term plan, you will reframe this work as McDonald's Work. This "pay-your-bills work" is not part of your identity but part of your plan. As such, you no longer need to think of your job with a sense of permanency. Be grateful that it provides financial benefits, but get ready to move onward.

Your biggest action-oriented step will be immersing yourself in Exploratory Work. This includes all the time, energy, and activities needed to discover your ideal career. Inexplicably, this work is not part of our school system. Few people engage in Exploratory Work when building their careers. It will be your secret weapon for career development.

From there, you will do what is necessary to gain access to your Path of Abundance, be it further training or starting on the lowest rung of your preferred career ladder. This Pay-Your-Dues Work requires the wisdom to know that character-building work is part of the journey.

If you are already in a career, you will decide whether your work needs rejuvenation, relaunching, or reinvention. Can you increase your happiness and success within a path that has not yet lead to either? Rejuvenation involves the least transactional costs so should, at least, be considered. You might decide to relaunch by staying in your general field but moving to a different company or heading to graduate school. And, yes, many of you will want the "out of the box" move promised by reinvention.

To move forward, you will need to get around the psychological blocks to career success. You'll understand that seemingly endless career options lead to the perils of choice; assuming that your career choice will be discovered naturally creates the "It will come to me" fallacy;

you'll need to learn techniques to overcome analysis paralysis and deal with ambiguity; and that you need to prioritize your needs and desires to avoid falling into the "I want it all" trap.

You will also need to grapple with fear as the foundational block for all of the aforementioned challenges, as well as anxiety related to financial insecurity, public embarrassment, and disappointing yourself.

You will now be ready to go onto your path and will do so by first analyzing the opportunity cost of staying at your current job. Every day you are spending doing something that you don't want to do costs you time that could be better spent. You might be overestimating your transactional costs related to whatever challenges need to be overcome to move from your current career to a better one.

You will further engage in situational analysis in order to examine how opportunities are likely to play out in the real world.

The process may seem lengthy. It is. Writers who suggest otherwise are not practicing career counselors. They don't understand the messy realities of most career changers. Significant Exploratory Work is required to better understand the New World of Work, your inner self, and the potential career matches that will lead you to happiness and success. This book will provide a blueprint for that journey.

My own transformation from Old World of Work big city attorney to New World of Work education-entrepreneur forged an experiential understanding of the process required to create one's own unique career path. In 2002, I started The Learning Consultants, a company designed to help clients with their educational needs. The simple story: I felt that my calling was in education and I thought I could best make an impact through entrepreneurship. It sounds easy enough but only in retrospect. The journey was filled with psychological and practical hurdles. Nonetheless, I do recall the transformative moments when I resolved to pursue my own path. Sometimes I meet clients in our career-counseling programs at just the right time, and our discussion sparks the epiphany that makes them dramatically act on something to forever change their work lives. My hope is that this book will do the same for you.

Phase I: Get Ready

Gratitude

Revolution

Insights

Consider yourself incredibly lucky. This may seem increasingly difficult in our turbulent economy, but take the long view: you were born during the best time period in history for creating a career filled with happiness and success.

Work was pretty horrible for most people throughout human history. The most common occupations were small farmer (often a euphemism for peasant) and manual laborer, including slave. Back-breaking work, long day after long day—that was one's "career."

Our whining about commuting, office politics, and tough bosses would be looked upon with disbelief by our ancestors, who would have been happy simply to work indoors.

Work as a means of personal fulfillment was not possible for most. Indeed, this is still true in wide swaths of the world today. Being in the position to read this book makes you fortunate even by modern standards.

Yet this luck is dismissed by most of us. A couple of decades ago, I recall fully partaking in a gripe session with fellow law-firm associates about the tedious work we were assigned. One associate didn't complain. Later, I understood why. He was originally from a war-torn African country and was too gracious to chastise us. I can only imagine—with full embarrassment—what he thought of our overprivileged lives as we complained about the horrors of mundane legal work while sitting in our beautiful offices enjoying free gourmet food and the assistance of legal secretaries.

If you are reasonably young, then you are beyond lucky. You have the potential to create a work life that generates freedom, satisfaction, and wealth beyond the wildest expectations of most people even just one generation ago.

To do so, you will need to develop yourself in many ways. This book will focus on developing the one area that will guide you forever: your wisdom. The end result of building career wisdom? You will be in position to create a successful career based on your passion, do so with people you like, and lead a well-balanced life. Your work life will become a source of immense happiness. And you will do so at a far younger age than ever before in the history of the industrialized world.

Why is it important to start with gratitude? Moving toward something affirmatively will start you on your path with positive energy and expectation. I know that many readers are in a tough state, looking to escape a current work environment, find a career path, or just get a job. You will need a lot of energy to create your own path, and positivity goes a long way to generating such energy.

Moreover, during your deeper moments of clarity you might reflect on both the history of humankind and the full spectrum of people who currently walk the earth. You live in a thin slice of lucky people who can ponder career choice. Career choice was not a historical problem for the vast majority of people, because they had no choices: they were born into work from which there was no escape.

You have the freedom to strive for both happiness and success. The New World of Work will allow you to control your destiny far more than at any time before. That's why you should start with gratitude.

What Am I Going to Do When I Grow Up (Even if I'm Already Grown Up)?

Many of you want help answering that question. It plagues people in their thirties and forties just as often as it does young adults. Many want and expect a single answer, but most people in the New World of Work will develop general paths rather than precise answers about what they will do for the rest of their lives.

As you go through stages in life, certain themes will dominate your thoughts: entry into a specific industry, development of marketable skills, credential building, moneymaking, security focus, work and family balance, your meaning/purpose, and legacy building. You will need to figure out each work stage and how to position yourself for the next one. This might be a five- to ten-year plan that requires you to continually ask yourself "What am I going to do next?" This is different from the Old World of Work where the expectation was commitment to a forty-year career track. This New World of Work paradigm is both liberating and confusing. Through developing Intrapersonal and Entrepreneurial Wisdom, you will be positioned to understand your next best career move for any stage in life.

Career Wisdom Leads to Career Mastery
Mastery is another big picture concept without an action-based checklist for you to move through in a few hours. Instead, it is a process with a lengthy start up phase and continual incremental improvements needed thereafter.

My first company, The Learning Consultants, was built with a mission to help our student clients reach their potential, with the view that mastery is the process by which to do so. Our most popular program, Student Mastery, teaches students how to master the job of student. By shifting the motivation of our students to higher levels and then training them in all aspects of study skills, class participation, and test taking, we bring students closer to mastering their student-job. In forming our career counseling programs, we created Career Mastery, which was similarly built around the mastery concept. Career Mastery starts with the subject of this book: Career Wisdom. From there, training in areas of skill development, among other areas, leads our clients to happy and successful careers.

The master's journey takes time. Moreover, unlike areas where development of identifiable and concrete skills and/or knowledge provides the key to mastery, development of wisdom is more complicated because wisdom is a nebulous concept.

Wisdom is the Answer
My career-coaching work usually involves helping clients answer an educational or career question. The clients wanting answers to specific career questions may have come to figure out whether they should leave their job, start a business, get more training or switch their college major. In our work together, we figured out what was best, and they left satisfied that they had an answer.

Other clients came in with despair. They expressed having no idea what to do for a career, or they had a career but were unhappy. Either way, such clients felt lost or trapped. In our work together, something clicked and they gained deeper personal awareness and/or a better understanding of the work world. They not only had an answer to whatever question prompted them to meet, but the wisdom to find future answers. Those clients who developed the wisdom and self-awareness to answer current and future questions inspired this book. Teach a person to fish…

The Power of Wisdom

Wisdom has a lasting quality that makes it superior to knowledge and an intuitive depth that surpasses the value of intelligence. Knowledge is necessarily ephemeral given our rapidly changing world. Facts about careers are ever shifting. Intelligence, at least as we commonly define it, does not necessarily reflect the ability to make good judgments about major life issues—math wizards are no better at career analysis than math phobics.

Career Wisdom

There are two subcategories of Career Wisdom.

Intrapersonal Wisdom: This is wisdom related to your internal life and is the key to finding happiness at work. Why are so many people unhappy at work? Most did not spend sufficient time figuring out their best-suited career path. This book's focus will be the inner wisdom needed to decipher what type of work will make you happy.

Entrepreneurial Wisdom: This is wisdom related to navigating the external world in order to ensure practical success and is meant far more broadly than simply the wisdom required to start a business. Those who act with Entrepreneurial Wisdom take control of their world: they figure out how the work world functions then optimally navigate their career path.

Combining Wisdoms to Find the Right Fit

Developing Intrapersonal Wisdom (happiness focused) plus Entrepreneurial Wisdom (success focused) will enable you to find work that will lead to happiness and success. It should be noted that there is no such thing as "one fit." A Venn diagram illustrating all work that could make you successful and all work that could make you happy would have an overlap leading to several different career possibilities. Your task is to find something within that area based on your unique preferences and skills.

Getting the Most Out of This Book

This book will be more helpful for those who want to make their work connected to something beyond just making a living. If you are solely interested in figuring out how to maximize income or power or any other measure of outward success while only giving lip service to wanting your work to generate happiness, then other resources are more suitable.

Here's what I mean about lip service: Years ago, during a job interview with a big Washington, DC, law firm, I asked a question about work/family balance. Two partners emphatically claimed that family was most important and that they strived to place family first. It turned out that one travelled two hundred and twenty days of the year, and the other would routinely say that the "real work begins after five o'clock." I hope family was their first priority, but they did not live their lives in a way that reflected that value. Be honest with yourself. If you simply want to know how to succeed in a practical sense, find books on how to do so in finance, politics, or technology. Go conquer Wall Street, Washington, DC, or Silicon Valley.

This book is also not for those who seek to live their dream without thoughts of practicality. As a fellow idealist, I salute your intentions, but I'm not interested in aiding the creation of more starving artists. If you believe that thoughts of practicality will dim your artistic mojo, put down this book, spend ten thousand hours cultivating your creative skills, and several thousand more hours marketing yourself. [1]

Furthermore, many young idealists want to be "pure," as in exclusively seeking to serve the world, without thoughts of worldly success. Seeking success for success's sake can seem disconcertingly ambitious for those who seek purposeful, fulfilling work. If you are not successful, however, you won't serve anyone. You will help the world by being successful enough to share your gifts with as many people as possible.

Although this book will help you decide where to direct your energies and effectively navigate the real world of work, it is not a "how to get a job" book. Entrepreneurial Wisdom will help you craft a networking plan, tailor cover letters, and customize your resume, but there will be no details in this book on how to do so.

Intrapersonal Wisdom will help guide you to the areas you need to develop in order to obtain happier work, but there will be no specific recommendations on how to journal, visualize, meditate, or any other activity designed to increase inner wisdom.

Finally, like all career books, merely reading this book without reflection and accompanying action will not give you the answer to what you should do for your career. It is my hope that this book will be one of many that lead you to greater wisdom along your path to a happy and successful career.

---

1 Ten thousand hours is the magic number to develop mastery, according to Malcolm Gladwell, among many others. See his book *Outliers*.

Entrepreneurial Wisdom: Understanding the New World of Work

You Are In a Revolution. You Just Didn't Notice.

To develop Entrepreneurial Wisdom, you have to understand the world as it is. Are you stuck with a work mind-set from the twentieth century? It turns out that the start of the twenty-first century was momentous not simply because of the change of millennium, but because it coincided with a work revolution.

Some revolutions are subtle. Eighteenth-century farmers were not calling the seeds of industrialization a "revolution" since it was actually a seventy-five-plus-year gradual transition. Those who were tilling their land likely heard about the advent of factories and machines. They could not have expected that everything about the practical world was about to change. It was a given that their children would take over the farm, so they had no reason to provide career advice. Indeed, they likely gave positively misguided advice based on experience from their soon-to-be-outdated way of work life. Their children entered the rapidly changing work world with expectations that their way of life would be the same as it was for their parents.

Before you think that modernity will keep you one step ahead of those ill-informed farmers, you might note that American autoworkers in the late twentieth century commonly advised their children that they could skip college and embrace lifetime employment in the automotive industry. It was only a few years ago that many parents urged their children to aim for secure employment in large corporations.

We have been undergoing and are continuing to undergo a work revolution that is potentially on the same scale as the Industrial Revolution in terms of affecting individual work lives. Most everyone who first heard about the Internet and e-mail in the late twentieth century was oblivious to the onslaught of change, just as those nineteenth-century farmers had been. For this reason, most parents today are in the same position as those parent-farmers—they have no idea how to advise their children about the New World of Work. Moreover, most of today's workers are in the same position as all those who relied on an agrarian economy for their living as the march of industrialization began changing their understanding of what the future held.

The New World of Work Revolution

In the Old World of Work, the path was predictable: graduate from college; find first job in chosen career field with perhaps a move or two to find the right organization; and then a long-time stay at that organization. Even the somewhat aimless or initially misdirected would usually find their career traction sometime in their mid to late twenties.

When I give talks on this subject, I often mention that when I graduated college in 1989, most anyone with decent grades from a decent college would find a decent job. I see heads nodding for anyone who graduated college before the mid-2000s.

Furthermore, career paths for most were predictable, particularly for those in the world of organizations. Upon joining a company in an entry-level position, one would strive for upward mobility. Career paths could easily be viewed on an organizational chart: assistant manager to associate manager to senior manager to assistant director to associate director and so on. There was a reasonable amount of predictability about moving through each of these points within three to seven years. Upward mobility would continue for some and stop for others.

Moving to a different department within the same company was considered a big career move. Taking a similar job in a different company was a huge—and somewhat risky—career move. Those who switched careers were considered highly unusual, often not in a good way. Those in professions or other specialized fields had their own paths, but for the most part those paths were similarly predictable.

For those in large, reasonably stable organizations who have not yet felt the sting of job disruption, the illusion of the Old World of Work remains. The misconception stems from not realizing that the pact of committing oneself to a corporation in exchange for secure employment into the indefinite future no longer exists. For workers who have experienced the effects of the New World of Work, thoughts of lifetime employment have already faded away.

This Is Not about Recent Economic Challenges

The financial tailspin of the first decade of the twenty-first century accelerated—but did not cause—the dramatic structural shifts that were already happening in the economy. Changes were afoot well before 2008's meltdown. The Internet revolution of the 1990s both decimated and created entire industries. In 1989, Charles Handy's seminal book, *The Age of Unreason*, predicted that organizations would contract to the smallest core of full-time workers possible then hire "just in time" workers as needed. His Nostradamus-like forecast correctly spotted the now commonplace corporate strategy of reducing labor costs whenever such a move serves the interest of the core corporate leadership.

On the flip side, employees would also have more freedom. "Free-agent nation," epitomized by successful freelancers, held the promise of greater worker autonomy.[2] It also further eroded the notion of long-term employment with single organizations.

In his 2005 book, *The World Is Flat*, Thomas Friedman described the new interconnectedness of the global economy as having both fantastic and frightening possibilities: worldwide business opportunities also brought worldwide

---

2 *Free Agent Nation* is one of Daniel Pink's excellent books.

labor eager to work for little pay. You could sell goods to the giant markets of China and India. Eager and talented workers in such places could also do your work at a fraction of the cost.

The Great Recession exacerbated all the negative aspects of these macroeconomic changes. There were far more jobs outsourced than new business opportunities created; far more jobs killed by technology than birthed; and far more secure jobs cut than jobs quit by self-selected freelancers. For this reason, the tsunami of economic change has been viewed primarily through a fearful lens.

But it need not be. Imagine if you had lived at the dawn of the Industrial Revolution and fully embraced what was then a massive transformation in the way people worked, or if you were one of the first to see how computers and the Internet could change everything. If you are on the ground floor of a new movement, then you might be on board for a spectacular rise. Guess what. You are.

Intrapersonal Wisdom: Understanding You

We have freedom to choose our career paths. That should lead to many happy workers. How then do people choose work that leads to unhappiness with such regularity? Just like you have to learn to navigate the world as it is, you have to learn to navigate yourself as you are. Sounds easy, yet it is not. The inner road to self-discovery is surprisingly confounding.

Unhappy work lives of knowledge-economy workers are dissimilar to the unhappy work lives of sweatshop workers; the latter have life circumstances that significantly curtail choice. While knowledge-economy workers have some limiting re-straints in relation to abilities and resources, they, ultimately, choose whatever career they want to pursue.

While we are individually responsible for our own well-being, there are several systemic reasons for the perva-siveness of career mismatches:

(1) We choose when we are too young.

When we decide our college major or choose our first job, we are too young to have the wisdom to choose properly. We don't know ourselves well enough. We definitely don't sufficiently understand the world of work.

(2) The knowledge economy is extraordinarily complex.

Prior to the Industrial Revolution, most young adults knew about the world of work—at least within their intended profession—because they worked with their parents, apprenticed with someone else, or were trained in a skill. Their world of work was comprehensible because the landscape of jobs was limited and far more tangible. In broad strokes, if you weren't a farmer, you would apprentice in a trade or become a merchant of some sort. Today, the intangible nature of most knowledge-based work—imagine explaining search engine optimization to a seventeenth-century blacksmith—makes it difficult for young people to sufficiently understand the present work world.

(3) Our education system utterly fails in providing opportunities for career exploration.

Our school systems can, and maybe someday will, do a better job of educating students about the real world of work. At the moment, the curriculum of our school systems is a mismatch with the realities of the work world.

You cannot control these systemic issues, but you can control how you understand your inner world and how that understanding can lead you to choose your optimal career path.

Key Intrapersonal Insights

Start by recognizing that solving the career puzzle is extraordinarily difficult. By doing so, you will commit to investing the time and energy to find answers.

Compare answering factual questions. A simple procedure (i.e., a Google search), pure objectivity (if the question is exclusively factual), quick solvability, and minimal meaningfulness of outcome make the solving process easy. In comparison, career choice has undefined processes for exploration, a high subjective to objective data ratio, no distinct time line (no deadline), and highly significant consequences. That combination makes career choice vexing.

What I call "key insights" will lead you to answers, but there is no single process for developing these insights. Some common practices follow.

Reading: Will this book move you toward a big-picture understanding of your career? I hope so. But you will need to read multiple books to develop key insights. *What Color Is Your Parachute?* is a classic—perhaps *the* classic career book—but for some reason it did not do much for me. That does not mean I won't recommend the book. Plenty of people think it's great. *Man's Search for Meaning*, Viktor Frankl's account of his days in a concentration camp, actually had a bigger impact on my career direction, even though it overtly has nothing to do with career counseling. Its key insight for me? Build a meaningful life through purposeful work that helps others. Maybe you'll read (or reread) *The Catcher in the Rye* and decide you no longer want to be a phony. This might prompt you to abandon the world of corporate façades.

Reflection: Do you have to imitate Thoreau and spend time alone walking in the woods? Meditate? Go for a long walk? Write in your journal? Each of us has our own process. Socrates's mandate, "The unexamined life is not worth living," may be extreme, but it's not a stretch to say that most people spend little time in genuine reflection.

To gain key career insights, carve out some regularly scheduled time for big-picture reflection. Don't expect instant results. Those who tell me they tried to meditate but it didn't work are no different from those who played tennis for the first time and declared that they couldn't play. Reflection leads to intuition. By its very nature, intuition cannot be forced. Put processes into place, and insights will come at unexpected times.

Expert Advisors: Malcolm Gladwell provides a brilliant treatise on the value of expertise in his book, *Blink*. Through numerous anecdotes, he describes how experts can spend a remarkably short amount of time solving seemingly intractable problems. Expert career counselors should lead you to key insights.

Why are top advisors so likely to provide key insights? Our brains work effectively through the understanding of patterns. Watch elementary school children play soccer. Pure chaos. A few years later, they play the game with structure. Based on past patterns, the kids now know where to run. Likewise, great coaches can tell players the specific area they need to work on to improve their game. In doing so, the coach is leveraging her understanding of the thousands of patterns she has observed. Seeking out a mentor in your current field of exploration or a career coach, informal or otherwise, works similarly.

Experiential Processes: Internships, job shadowing, and informational interviewing are more likely to lead to deep career insights than any other process. The challenge, of course, is that you have to first know what you might want to do before you set up such experiences. In addition, experiences such as internships take an enormous amount of time.

What can be done right now?

Personality Theory:
The Shortcut to Intrapersonal Wisdom

Years ago, I worked with Jill. She was older than me and was one of my first career-counseling clients. I was not yet an expert counselor but I had a deep knowledge of personality-profiling tools. The Myers-Briggs Type Indicator, the most well-known personality test in the corporate world, is the hero of this story.

Jill had come to see me because she was miserable in her work as a medical biller. I had her complete the Myers-Briggs test, and her result was ENFP (**E**xtraverted, i**N**tuitive, **F**eeling, and **P**erceiving). In broad strokes, this meant that Jill drew energy from the outside world (E), which usually translates to preferring to work with people than work solo. Jill was a big-picture thinker (N) who would not enjoy deeply detailed work. She liked making decisions based on human implications and not in an impersonal manner (F), and was someone who preferred a flexible routine (P)—a nonroutine—who would resent a highly structured environment.

As a medical biller, Jill generally worked alone, dealt with the minutia of detailed coding, and made impersonal decisions in a highly structured office environment—quite the opposite of what her personality test suggested would suit her.

Why had she been in this field for so long? When she was younger, Jill was told that healthcare would be a booming industry, but a mediocre academic background and the thought of blood scared her away from direct medical care.

So Jill started her career in medical billing as the lowest hanging fruit on the healthcare tree. As it goes with many first-time workers, she had no basis from which to compare her job to others. When she complained to her parents, their standard response was, "Work is not supposed to be enjoyable. That's why it's work."

Resigned to low expectations for career happiness, she spent her first three years in the workforce unhappy, but not quite miserable enough to make a change. In addition, while her coworkers were nice, they were older and different than Jill and thus she had a hard time developing friendships at work, an important issue for Feelers in the Myers-Briggs framework.

Jill had a friend who helped get her a job at another doctor's office. The thought of working with her friend in a different environment appealed to Jill. She applied and got her new job. The enjoyment of working with a friend was enough to make the first few months of the job better.

But soon the actual work of the job created the same sense of dullness and dread of getting up on Mondays for work. Yet again, the work wasn't terrible enough to quit, so she did what she was "supposed to do." Since her energy was consumed at home—she had gotten married and had two children during this time—she spent almost no time engaging in Exploratory Work. Ten years passed.

Between the two jobs, Jill had now spent thirteen years of her life doing something that she was entirely ill suited to do. She felt a split life—happy and purposeful at home but unhappy and purposeless at work.

With her children a bit older, Jill was in a better state to change. She felt that forty hours per week doing something she did not like, plus the dreary after-work feelings about her job, compelled her to make what she considered a radical decision—she would leave the doctor's office.

Unfortunately, Jill's experience was only in medical billing, and the jobs that appealed to her required credentials that she did not have. She was advised that her medical billing experience was useful to health insurance companies. The human resource recruiter at the company that eventually hired Jill relayed that some of their internal billing code auditors had moved into other areas, such as the marketing department, and served on committees evaluating whether holistic healthcare remedies could be covered by insurance.

Jill's thought processes swirled with thoughts of holistic healthcare (a field focused on helping people, a Feeler's field), marketing (big-picture creativity, an Intuitive's desire), and options to do other things (a Perceiver's need). She felt something stir in her soul in a way that she never had before at work.

But Jill's desperation to leave her current situation made her confuse possibility with reality. She was hired to review medical coding, and while she did have a different work environment, the contours of this job were not entirely different from her previous one. In addition, her boss was a detail-oriented, highly structured person who jumped all over Jill for missing small—and in Jill's mind insignificant—details and not abiding by corporate procedures.

Jill noted that her boss likely had a different Myers-Briggs type. As an important aside, understanding personality theory provides a significant added benefit of better understanding others, be it coworkers or family members.

Jill's subpar reviews squashed any thoughts of transferring to a different department, and she didn't want to anyway as she had grown to despise the stifling corporate environment. She hung on in misery for another three years.

The strange truth that hits many unhappy midcareer workers reached Jill: it was unfortunate that her first jobs in medical billing were not quite bad enough to make her quit. If she had her current job years ago, Jill would likely have been emotionally compelled to invest in Exploratory Work in order to find a more suitable career.

When Jill and I met, she had no idea what she wanted to do. She laughed when she heard that one of the clear conclusions from the Myers-Briggs test was that she should not be a medical biller.

Jill wondered what would have happened had someone given her this test long ago. How come no one ever told her how ill suited she was for this work? How could she have wasted sixteen years of her work life? Someone could have simply given her this test and she would have concluded she was not suited for such work.

I don't want to leap to the happy ending of this story without noting that six months of soul-searching, money-related worrying, career research, and situational analysis transpired first. But soon enough, Jill found part-time work in a naturopathic physician's office very close to home in order to pursue work in the holistic healthcare field. She started getting trained in a specific alternative-treatment discipline and taking entrepreneurial marketing classes. When we last were in contact, her career was in the right field (holistic healthcare), using her preferred ways of working (big-picture thinking, helping people), and in the right situation (a nonstructured small environment).

Personality Testing Leverages Patterns: Much like an expert career counselor leverages past patterns, proper application of quality personality tests does the same. If those with your personality type generally detest the career you are considering, you should proceed with extreme caution, or at least be highly aware of the issues that will likely challenge you. Many a miserable career could have been avoided and many a happy career found with a proper understanding of career personality profiling.

To skeptics, I note that the Internet has ruined personality tests for many—clicking on a test that promises an answer to a major life question almost universally leads to test-taker disappointment. Your future spouse won't be found through a test, nor will your future career. These charlatan sites should not diminish the validity of every personality-profiling tool. Even the best tests do not provide answers. Instead, these tests provide data. That data is useful only if turned into helpful information, and then actionable only if the information is turned into good advice.

If you take a career-profiling personality test, expect that you will be gathering data and, with hope, key insights. You will not get answers. "I had no idea what I wanted to do for a career. I took a test and now I know." That doesn't happen. If it did, the test would be worth the price of a college education.

Prior to meeting me, Rich had taken a career inventory test that provided recommendations regarding careers to explore. The results ranged from machine operator to sales rep to airline pilot. He complained that such expansive recommendations were not helpful. I responded that the data needed to be transformed into actionable information.

Rich had come to us because of his ambivalence about leaving his secure job in the insurance industry. He was very unhappy in his current work. However, his coworkers with the same job chided him for complaining, as they liked the work. They had convinced him to stay put.

I explained that being stuck in an office staring at insurance data all day was not torturous to Rich's coworkers. I guessed that many of them probably liked the data analysis and detailed review required for the job. Personality-preference tests would likely reveal that they enjoyed the secure feelings of staying in one place and performing tasks with distinct expectations. They probably felt comfortable and confident mastering a job that required excellence in repetition. Security in both structure and activities would likely be important for them. Rich's test results showed that he needed a more action-oriented job. If he didn't leave, his life would be sucked out from him. While the career test did not give him the answer to what job he should take, it did give him a key insight as to what criteria would be critical for career happiness.

Personality test results are useful, as opposed to merely fun, only if you know how to turn the data into helpful information and subsequently use it for guidance, or if someone with expertise can provide the same. Simply put, personality tests should be starting, not finishing, points.

I'll occasionally read a critical piece about career tests and invariably discover that the article is written not by a counseling practitioner, but by a writer who has never worked in the field. I can report a great deal of success in deriving key insights from having worked with some of the more well-known personality-profiling tests. More importantly, many of my clients cursed the fact that they did not pay attention to personality theory earlier in their life.

Personality Tests to Consider
When understood and applied properly, some personality systems can provide excellent revelations. The tests that I have used are below, and simple web searches will lead you to plentiful resources on each. My brief overview of these tests provides a starting point, but your task is to try whichever tests appeal to you, gather data, and then begin the real work of unlocking key career insights. I elaborate on Myers-Briggs not because it is the best, but because it is the most prevalent.

Myers-Briggs Test Indicator: This test has become well known throughout the world of human talent management. It covers four sets of personality preferences, each measured along a continuum. If you are like most people, you will find yourself somewhere in the middle of the continuum but more aligned to one side than the other.

For example, the first variable—Extraversion (E)–Introversion (I)—determines whether you focus predominantly on your outer world or your inner world. If you prefer to focus on the outer world, you are an E. If you prefer to focus on your inner world, you are an I.

If the test posed only a single question—do you focus more on your outer or inner world?—many people would respond that it depends on the situation. Fortunately, the test has enough questions to establish your preference, even if slight. Someone with a high E tendency might present as perpetually engaged with others or immersed in worldly activities. Someone with a high I tendency might present as the bookish sort who chooses solitary activities or socialization only with close friends. Those in the middle would be hard to decipher from the outside.

Those who focus more on information coming from their five senses are Sensors (S), and those who prefer to interpret meaning through patterns and possibilities are Intuits (N). Sensates tend to be more down to earth and factually attuned, and Intuitives tend to be more big-picture and theoretically focused. I am fairly confident that the vast majority of accounting majors are Sensors and the vast majority of philosophy majors are Intuitives.

Those who make decisions primarily through objective, impersonal lens are Thinkers (T), and those who do so primarily through examining the consequences to people are Feelers (F). This does not relate to intellect, but rather decisional preference. For example, when I was a criminal prosecutor in Philadelphia, I argued cases before judges of equal smarts, but who decided similar cases dissimilarly. Judge Thinker was by the book. The letter of law mattered. He would say, "My hands are tied by the law when I make decisions." The unique human circumstances of the case would take a backseat to consistency, justice, and as literal a read of the law as possible. Judge Feeler was more attuned to the individuals involved. The letter of the law could be stretched to get a fair result for those in the particular case. He would say, "My interpretation of the spirit of the law leads me to my decision."

Those who are decisive, take deadlines seriously, are comfortable with structure, and like to get their work done before playing tend to be Judgers (J). Those who feel better with options open, have a more elastic view of time constraints, are more comfortable without structure, and like to get their playing done before work tend to be Perceivers (P).

If you have taken a career personality-profiling test, it was likely Myers-Briggs. You might remember your "type" in the form of four-letter combinations such as ENFP or ISTJ. At the very least, the test results provide baseline information to understand what activities and situations you prefer. Each of the single variables might provide interesting information that could lead to key insights, but the real power of the test is the combination of the variables. An ISTJ (Introvert, Sensor, Thinker, Judger) usually appears to be analytical and a bit rigid, whereas its variable opposite, an ENFP (Extravert, Intuitive, Feeler, Perceiver), tends to generate many ideas but lacks follow-through.

Even two-letter combinations make a difference. Intuitive Feelers (NF), for example, are known as idealists. I noticed that a disproportionate number of my clients are NFs, even though NFs are relatively rare in the general populace. I then realized that not only are NFs more likely to be seekers of something more ideal—and thus found a career-counseling website—but that my writing on the site appealed to idealists because I write from the perspective of an ENFJ (Extravert, Intuitive, Feeler, Judger).

RIASEC: Each letter or code stands for a particular type: **R**ealistic (Doer), **I**nvestigative (Thinker), **A**rtistic (Creator), **S**ocial (Helper), **E**nterprising (Persuader), and **C**onventional

(Organizer). Based on the work of psychologist John Holland.

The Strong Interest Inventory: This is a more elaborate version of Holland's codes, as it includes the same RIASEC findings, but adds basic interest, occupational, and personal styles findings.

Five Factors: Sometimes called The Big Five Personality Factors, this test measures openness, conscientiousness, extraversion, agreeableness, and neuroticism.

The Enneagram: This test measures nine types of core motivations. I find this to be the most psychologically penetrating of all tests. But it is also the most complicated and requires significant interpretation.

For those of you who find personality theory helpful, I would encourage using any of the above tests to gain key insights. For those dismissive of personality theory, there are plenty of other ways to develop Intrapersonal Wisdom. Use whatever methods best suit you.

Phase II: Get Set

Three Paths

Vision Creation

Happiness and Success

The Three Paths

The New World of Work has led to three general career paths:

The Path of Abundance: Careers on this path are marked by great fortune both economically and psychologically, with vast opportunities for extraordinarily enjoyable and fulfilling work, along with optimal work-life balance, happiness, and success.

The Path of Struggle: Careers on this path are marked by job instability, more time spent earning less real income than previous generations, and happiness and success attained at great sacrifice.

The Path of Disaster: Work lives on this path do not develop into real careers, but are characterized by unhappy work activities and lack of work success. Financial independence is out of reach and neither happiness nor success is found.

Let's start with the good news.

The Path of Abundance

The Path of Abundance may sound like the beginning of a crazed self-help infomercial.[3] And it would be, if I were writing about the future of work for most people. Nevertheless, you are likely in a position to have work so great that it doesn't feel like work. Why? Because you are reading this book. This means you are likely living somewhere in the industrialized Western world and in the position to ponder career choice. You are probably college educated and likely came from an upper-middle-class socioeconomic background. Or, you are the type of person who has taken the initiative to build your career, despite more challenging circumstances than most readers of this book, so your good fortune is that you are wired to strive for a better life. That's all you really need.

You could earn enough money to feel fully secure while doing what you love. You can gain freedom from the constraints of the Old World of Work through gaining autonomy and control of time. You could be excited about going to work.

---

3 I feel compelled to provide some context about my background. I was heavily cultured in the worlds of skepticism and scientific-mindedness. Having a father with a scientific background, being trained as an attorney (specifically as a criminal prosecutor), and, as I say with some literalness, growing up amid harsh New Jersey cynicism, I am ever mindful of making claims that lack clear and convincing proof.

Despite the marketing-infused title, "abundance" definitely does not promise four-hour work weeks while you accumulate millions of dollars doing what you love. Initially, you will need to work to pay your bills while you engage in Exploratory Work to decide what to do for your next step; then, after you have figured it out, be willing to pay your dues on your upward path. This may translate to working at a job that you do not like, while you take an online class to build your skills and seek out part-time work at the entry level of your chosen field.

Initially, you will likely need to work forty-plus hours, you may need to defer making substantial income while you build your career, and you might not love your work. But your efforts will be worth it if you get on your correct path.

Getting you on your path—what I call the Path of Abundance—is the goal. I define that path as work that leads you to feel both happy and successful. This is not a modest goal. Feeling happy at work would put you in the minority—about 10 to 15 percent.[4] While there are no statistics to determine what slice of this happy group also feels successful, a reasonably conservative estimate is that 3 to 5 percent are happy while at work, but are not thriving financially or in other ways defined as practically successful.

That leaves about 10 percent that are leading work lives on the Path of Abundance. Books that set up hyperbolic goals are at best inspiring in the short term but deflating in the long term (does it really take just seven simple steps to make millions in passive income so that you can travel the world while not working?). Those who live such realities

---

4 See Gallup-Forbes poll, March 25, 2014.

are an even thinner slice than the 1 percent. Being in the top 10 percent of the work force is reasonably attainable for anyone who has the character to seek out and read this type of book.

Your first step will involve creating a vision for what you consider happiness and success. Vision creation requires clarity. The terms "happy" and "successful" are vague and often mixed together. I will define each with greater precision. If you prefer a simple definition, you can call career success all the practical things that emanate from work. For most, this amounts to money and prestige. You can call career happiness all the idealistic things that stem from doing work you enjoy and that feeds your soul.

The Path of Abundance Serves as an Affirmative Motivational Force

While we could focus upon the misfortunes of farmers and others whose way of life was destroyed in the meteor storm of industrialization, we also could consider the extraordinary opportunities created by the Industrial Revolution. Beyond Rockefeller, Mellon, and Ford, there were tens of thousands of entrepreneurs and business executives who grew quite wealthy during this time. More importantly, there were millions whose quality of life was substantially upgraded, leading to the strong middle class that propelled the Western world through the twentieth century.

Similarly, while the economic pain resulting from unpredictability and work chaos has challenged and will continue to challenge many, if you understand how to expertly develop and position yourself, you will be able to navigate a wonderful path toward abundance. Chaos creates opportunity.

There is more good news. Idealists almost always desire freedom. The turbulent forces of the New World of Work have unshackled workers from the confines of decades spent working within a single organization. In past generations, those who were not tethered to corporate structures risked damage to their resumes. This is increasingly not the case. Indeed, as the New World of Work moves toward a looser entrepreneurial/freelancer/free agent structure, those who have stayed only in large organizations will be at greater risk because they won't know how to generate their own income.

Envision what your Path of Abundance would encompass. For some, this will entail making as much money as possible (abundance of wealth). For idealists, wealth accumulation is often a part of a philanthropic plan. For others, it will be creating enough passive income to create freedom (abundance of time). For those in search of meaning, it will be creating purposeful work (abundance of fulfillment). For all, there will be some unique combination of the above along with other areas of desire (fun, creativity, autonomy, to name a few.)

If you are an idealist seeking to make a positive difference, you should be ecstatic about the career opportunities awaiting you. There has never been a more opportune time for an individual to create change. You could film a video in the morning, post it in the afternoon, and have it go viral that night. While a business idea or a career opportunity will not work at such warp speed—at least not yet—you have a real opportunity to change the world.

True, we are in the midst of economic/work/job disorder. But this is a great thing for those who do not want to wait in line or navigate an established system. You can build your own job and create your own system.

You could develop a combination of outstanding skills, credentials, contacts, and work character to create a work life that is enjoyable, fulfilling, and prosperous.

You could have periods of deep creativity that may require several years of intense but engaging work. If you succeed, you will also have the choice—at a far younger age than ever before—to travel, engage passionately in your hobbies, spend time with your family, and live an ideal balance of work and personal life. You will have abundance of both time and money.

You might have so many creative, inspiring, interesting work projects that you'll choose to work intensely; partially for more money, but also for the challenge of reaching your human potential.

How could such a great work world exist? The boundaries that required the majority of idealists to let their ideas wither on the vine have mostly been broken down. There have always been people who had great ideas. In the organizational world of the twentieth century, however, capital was needed for office space, equipment, labor, inventory, and every other part of the infrastructure required to make a great idea become a reality.

Today and in the near future, you will need the intangibles of a great idea, excellent work character, strong communication and problem-solving skills, social connections, credentials to help make connections, and…that's about it. Other than a computer and a few other low-cost technology items, there is no longer a need for expensive infrastructure. You can create your own work reality on the very computer you might be using to read this book.

Since your work will emanate from your own ideas, the likelihood that you will be highly engaged and passionate about your work is higher than ever. In this new career reality, you could have enormous creative control over your work and personal life. Great fortune, both economically and psychologically, awaits you.

One caution, do not get intimidated by stories of those on the Path of Abundance who are in the Facebook/ Google/Twitter universe. The real inspiration stems from the millions of New World of Work idealists who are creating happy and successful careers out of the public spotlight.

Motivation Comes from Understanding the Other Paths
I've always been a hard-wired optimist. But my optimism has been tempered by decades of real-world observation: in this framework, the vast majority will not get on the Path of Abundance. Some people will have to deal with socio-economic challenges that will make even getting on the Path of Struggle a herculean task. If your mother is a drug addict and your father is in and out of jail, then just escaping that cycle of despair would be impressive. Health and relationship issues can also pose major challenges. The more general challenge, however, is not external but internal. Psychological blocks—mostly originating from fear—prevent many from striving to create optimal work lives.

While fear can stop people in their tracks, it can also propel people into motion. One of my closest friends and

DARYL CAPUANO

I often debate whether fear should be used as motivation. I am generally opposed to using anything negative to motivate. My friend has a more real-world sensibility about the use of fear as a motivational force. He argues that if people understand the potential downside, they will do their best to avoid that pain. He has a point. Showing someone the results of drunk driving is more effective than showing sober drivers arriving safely home.

Motivation Comes from Understanding the Consequences of Nonaction

The consequences of not acting affirmatively to build your career are far more dramatic than any time in recent history. In the post–World War II, pre–Great Recession era, even those who were not thriving usually had jobs. Following a conventional path was sufficient. I worked on an assembly line during the summer between high school and college. One of the older guys, Joe, advised me on my last day: "Keep your head straight, stay out of trouble, and you'll be all right." While we didn't discuss the underlying foundations of this advice, it seemed that Joe and many of the guys I worked with expected a predictable work life where one could do without big-picture career analysis. Stay within the lines and things should work out. Now the consequences of not developing career wisdom are potentially devastating.

The Path of Struggle

When I give presentations on the subject of the New World of Work, I'm excited by the prospect of inspiring audience members to strive for the possibility of creating a wonderful career. But the truth is that far more people in the Western world will be on the Path of Struggle.

The New World of Work has made job instability the norm. The macrofactors that once ensured long-term stability for those at large organizations have disappeared. In the not-so-old days, putting time into a company ensured job security. Laying off a long-term employee with a good record was a rarity. Now a management committee in New York can decide to terminate an entire department— your department—with minimal thought of the people in the group. The ten years you put in does not matter quite so much. Excessive focus on quarterly earnings, regular management turnover, and cost-cutting financial maneuvering makes the notion of secure jobs in large companies a mere illusion.[5]

---

5 I am a political independent and not prone to mob-generated populist sentiments. But I am stunned by the shamelessness of corporate CEOs who "earn" multimillion-dollar compensation packages from a stacked corporate board of friends, and simultaneously lay off workers because of short-term focus on quarterly earnings. Until shareholders revolt, corporations are no longer safe havens for steady jobs.

For those on the Path of Struggle, jumping from job to job because of outsourcing, downsizing, contract ending, company closing, and all other destabilizing economic shifts will be standard fare. A smaller portion of this struggling group will have what are considered good jobs and stable careers. But they will work extraordinarily hard to maintain a standard of living similar to that of their parents.

This group will include many professionals. Relatively speaking, this subgroup will be fine financially; they will simply make the trade that many generations have done before them—a lot of time for a lot of money. The new exchange rate, however, will not be as fortunate for workers as it was in the past.

Even for the talented, the globalization of the world's labor markets will deflate wages for most Westerners. The same forces that decimated the US manufacturing sector will soon do the same to the lower-level white-collar world. If a large accounting firm can hire a smart, hardworking non-American to crunch numbers for half the price, that is exactly what it will do. This path will swallow up many good people who followed the rules, did what they were told, and progressed down the standard path of getting good grades to get to a good college to get a solid job with a reputable company, and then worked hard for that company. It won't be their fault that the company implodes, lays off half its workforce, or is bought by another entity that strips it bare. But it is the responsibility of each one of us to keep up with the changing times and position ourselves for success in the knowledge economy.

The Path of Disaster

Some portion of those in the New World of Work will suffer deeply. They will suffer in a way that no other generation from the middle class has since the Great Depression. They will have long periods of unemployment interspersed with periods of unfulfilling work. They will likely need financial help from their parents well into their thirties. Thereafter, they will barely be able to sustain themselves, let alone a family of their own.

My first book, *Motivate Your Son*, covered in depth the topic of aimless twentysomethings. In simple summary, those walking the Path of Disaster will have developed neither sufficient work skills nor sufficient work character to compete in the knowledge economy.[6] Unlike prior generations where American (and Western) economic hegemony served as a reasonable fail-safe for underachievers, ruthlessly inexpensive worldwide competition for lower-paying white-collar jobs will devastate those without marketable skills.

You won't be on this path. Why? Because you are taking steps to ensure that you master the New World of Work.

---

6 While this book will not focus on blue-collar jobs, learning a trade would be the best generic advice I could give to those who are not trying to build a career in the knowledge economy.

Movement and Percentage on the Three Paths

Many people will float between these paths, not neatly compartmentalized on one path. Furthermore, there will be varying degrees of success and challenge for those who are on any of the paths. If only we could all have Oprah's spot on the Path of Abundance!

The percentage of people on each path cannot be neatly divided into thirds. The forces of economic change lead me to speculate that 10 percent will be on the Path of Abundance; 60 percent will be on the Path of Struggle, and—stunningly, by standards relative to modern Western economies—as many as 30 percent will be on the Path of Disaster.

Other than to provide a kick in the pants, there is no need to focus on the Paths of Struggle and Disaster. We'll focus on the Path of Abundance first by thinking about desired end results.

Vision Creation for Happiness and Success
What will make you happy?

"I want to like what I'm doing."

"I want to enjoy my work."

"I want to be happy."

So my clients tell me. I understand. I then ask:

"What work activities do you enjoy?"

"What gives you deep satisfaction?"

"What type of career would provide you meaning and purpose?"

Silence or half-thought-out answers follow. Given the consequences of these answers, it seems strange that most people have never thought through what specifically would make them happy at work. I can relate. When I was

24 and confident that my path would involve "making a difference" as an attorney, a high-minded but naïve and vague answer to the career question, Dr. James Spady, Penn's legendary Dean of the Fels School of Government, pressed me for concrete particulars: "Ok, you want to make a difference. How? What work do you actually want to do?" I replied "public service." He retorted "you don't know what the f--- you want to do." He was right.

What constitutes success?
   "I want to have enough money to do what I want."
   "I want to be free to have enough time to do what I want in my off hours."
   "I want to feel proud about what I do."
   I then ask:
   "What level of income would provide you with enough money?"
   "What amount of flexibility is required to pursue your personal interests?"
   "What type of work will provide enough prestige for you?"
   Again, silence usually follows. Spend time discovering the specific details that matter to you, as the answers will dictate your target. For example, when I was an enforcement attorney with the Securities and Exchange Commission in Washington, DC, I would occasionally talk with the highly affluent witnesses who were entangled in the multi-million dollar frauds we were investigating. On the subject of money, I heard phrases such as: "I want to be airplane rich" and "He who dies with the most toys wins." While their values were pathetic, they sure had clarity! Idealists usually have far less certain financial targets and, therefore, wind up unclear as to how

to navigate the work world in relation to their monetary goals.

Your goal should be to have enough knowledge to express your financial goals as did one of our recent clients: "I need $36,000 annually to meet my basic living expenses; $48,000 to have enough to spend on small luxuries like socializing and travel and $60,000 to also have enough to save for retirement." These specific numbers will become empowering on your journey.

Defining Happiness and Success from Work

Happiness and success are not usually well defined; neither term is clearly delineated from the other, causing career seekers to merge the definitions in ways that lead to great confusion. For the sake of speaking in common conversational form, I define the two terms as follows:

Happiness from Work: Your Internal Experience of Life While Working or Thinking about Working.
How do you feel when you are at work? If you feel good, then you are happy. If you feel bad, then you are not. At first glance, this seems easy enough. But there is more to happiness than simple enjoyment; for idealists, happiness also includes satisfaction, flow, and fulfillment. Understanding what will make you happy stems primarily from Intrapersonal Wisdom.

Success from Work: Your External Experience of Life Resulting from the Rewards of Your Work.
This includes all areas of life outside of actual work activities. Financial well-being is the easiest to understand. Control of time (freedom) and self-esteem (identity) are other areas. Understanding how to be successful stems primarily from Entrepreneurial Wisdom.

Conflating Happiness and Success

Happiness and success intertwine in a way that makes separating the two difficult. Those with good jobs, in a conventional sense, are not sure how to answer the question of whether they are happy in their work. A recent response from a client wonderfully illustrates this point: "Am I happy with my work? I am happy telling people I work for Goldman Sachs and happy with my compensation, but I feel like jumping out a window when I'm there."

The experience of conflating happiness with success is one that I know very well based on my experience working as an attorney. Many lawyers like being lawyers but do not enjoy doing legal work. I have heard variations of this theme from investment bankers (like the Goldman Sachs client), doctors, and top business executives. I should also note that work life encompasses not only the technical aspects of the job, but also the people, pressures, and hours required by the work. More than a few doctors have told me they like practicing medicine but have grown to detest their work lives because of all the aspects required outside of treating patients.

Happiness and Success Are Intertwined

The biggest challenge when trying to neatly divide happiness and success in career discussions is that there is no neat dichotomy between the two, and thus there will be some mixing of terms. Certainly your internal happiness at work affects how you experience life outside of work. Your good mood from your day job should spill over into your night life. It is equally true that you might feel happier at work because your job is prestigious or because you know you are making a lot of money, even if you dislike your actual work activities.

Nonetheless, people use these definitions too loosely and interchangeably, so try your best to untangle the two as you evaluate potential careers. If you hear someone say, "I'm happy with my job because I make enough money to vacation in Aspen and Martha's Vineyard," then unless the speaker continues that she is happy with her work activities, view her as successful but not happy. If you hear someone say "I am successful because I get to do what I want for work," but you know the speaker is unable to pay his bills, then he is happy but not successful.

Happy Work

Happiness at work encompasses a range of psychological states of satisfaction.

Simple Enjoyment. Do you enjoy what you do at work? Not what your work provides—like money—but your actual work day. If you can honestly answer yes, then congratulations, for you are in a small minority.

If you are a lifeguard at a swimming pool and your activities are confined to socializing, getting sun, and swimming, then you likely have enjoyable work. Similarly, if you are a social type who works for a good boss at a lively but not stressful company with coworkers who are also friends, then you probably enjoy your work day.

Eudaimonia. But those of you who have picked up this book are likely looking for something more ethereal than simple enjoyment. Aristotle may have captured the concept of work satisfaction best when he wrote about "eudaimonia." There is no perfect English translation, although "flourishing" seems closest. He noted that there is something beyond the simple notion of enjoyment that encompasses a human's satisfaction from work.

My college philosophy professor explained eudaimonia like this: "A painter is meant to paint. That's when he is most alive." Even if the artist does not appear to be enjoying himself, he is doing something aligned to his higher self that elicits satisfaction. His fully engaged creative energies elevate his spirit to its highest levels.

When workers of all sorts are creatively engaged—particularly when they have a great deal of autonomy—they experience eudaimonia. This is not confined to designers, writers, and artists; builders of any sort can experience it. Most entrepreneurs feel this way during the positive parts of building their business, as do corporate sales managers building their teams, and mathematicians creating statistical models.

Flow. More common in modern parlance, "flow," a term coined by noted psychologist and author Mihaly Csikszentmihalyi, describes work that energizes by demanding the full involvement of the worker in some psychologically satisfying way. The craftsman engaged in his trade might easily come to mind, but those who report satisfaction in all types of work can also attain flow. Indeed, Csikszentmihalyi's initial study and discovery of flow focused on workers in an assembly line. An engineer solving a thorny but intriguing problem or a graphic artist designing an intricate pattern both experience flow.

The sports world provides another way to describe flow. The cliché of being "in the zone" is used to describe someone performing at a different level than normal consciousness would seem to allow. One would hope that heart surgeons regularly attain this state, but anyone with work that engages concentration in some transcendent way can also be "in the zone."

Fulfillment. I separate the notion of fulfillment from the others because I can't imagine a hospice worker saying, "I was in the zone today." Fulfillment derived from the knowledge that your work is making a difference is a distinctly different feeling than one gets while engaged in enjoyable or flow-like activities. Medical workers, soldiers, and educators are perhaps the most obvious examples of those who derive fulfillment from their work even when performing activities that are not always enjoyable.

A counterexample will illustrate the distinction. I have many clients who are salespeople of one sort or another. They often report that they enjoy their work (simple enjoyment) but know that what they are doing is not particularly consequential (unfulfilling). Usually these clients are older and becoming more self-aware. They express that something is missing even if they enjoy the social interactions inherent in sales and the adrenal rush they receive when landing a big commission. Many do not know how to articulate their feelings of malaise. "I like sales. I'm good at it. I'm making a lot of money. But I don't know..." Ultimately they realized that they wanted to do something that had greater purpose.

To further separate fulfillment from mere enjoyment, I point to a few of my clients who work in the burgeoning green industry, a field designed to produce environmentally friendly products. They feel good about their work even if they do not fully enjoy their work activities. Environmental work is quite scientific. Some clients confess they don't really understand variations in carbon emissions levels and other terms of environmental consequence, but like knowing that the products they are creating and selling are helping the environment.

Of all the factors that guarantee happiness at work, fulfillment provides the best promise for providing work that will be psychologically satisfying. Having meaning and purpose in your work will allow you to sleep better and ready to go when you wake up.

Strategy: Vision Creation

What activities do you enjoy? And more precisely, which of these can be translated into activities that are rewarded by the marketplace?

What activities provide you a deep sense of satisfaction? Did you like creating multimedia projects? Leading a group in a brainstorming session? Writing for a school or company newsletter? Any activity that creates the elusive sense of eudaimonia?

Have you ever found yourself immersed in a work activity such that time seemed to pass by without notice? Flow is a cousin of eudaimonia, so it's likely these activities overlap.

Picture ending your career. What legacy do you want to leave? What gave you fulfillment, meaning, and purpose?

As you chart your Path of Abundance, consider whether your chosen career could lead to some combination of simple enjoyment, eudaimonia, and/or fulfillment. Create your thematic vision around what matters most to you.

Should I Just Focus on Happiness?

Some of my creative clients are blocked because they have bought in fully to the half-clever maxim "Do what you love and the money will follow." Doing what you love increases your chances of success—that's the clever part. The missing half is that within the variety of things that you love (though "like" is more realistic), only some will have a sufficient market for you to earn enough money to be successful. Moreover, you have to be good enough in your field to get rewarded by the market. The size of your target market along with the level of skill (luck, connections, and resources included) determines whether doing what you love will lead to a successful career.

Writers who blithely advise others to follow their passion are rarely practicing career counselors. Marsha Sinetar wrote the book *Do What You Love and The Money Will Follow* in 1989. It's a fine book, but was written in a very different time period. The 1980s until the dawn of the Internet age might be viewed historically as the apex of corporate job stability. It would not be a stretch to say that those who were college educated or union affiliated during this time period could choose a path that would ensure a stable career. The trade-off for stability, however, was often the bulk of a career spent in a narrowly defined prism. This exchange was often ill suited for idealists because the corporate grid stifled individuality, creative energy, and work dreams.

The "love your work" advisory trend was an excellent way to counterbalance the prior generation's programming to stay in the matrix. As with most reactionary movements, the needle went too far in the opposite direction since too many readers focused exclusively on the "do what you love" notion. The fine print—mentioned by most writers but lost on most readers—is that for the money to follow, you must develop marketable skills, navigate the marketplace to get hired, and deal with mundane aspects of work life.

Passion Seekers Must Master Practicality

Your passions can be rewarded only if you put in the time and energy to master the practical world. Three common markers of success—financial well-being, freedom, and high self-esteem—illustrate the point.

Clients who express dismay that their businesses are not generating sufficient income will describe their passion and happiness around their work, but then lament that the business has become an enormous challenge in every other area of their lives. It's hard to love your work day knowing you can't pay the rent.

Long-time aspiring actors might wait tables forty hours a week, go on countless auditions in order to work the occasional acting gig, and are presumably happy while acting. But they are not successful given their limited freedom. Paying one's dues is necessary, but a decade of chasing a dream wears down most everyone. Marty Nemko, a well-known career counselor and writer in San

Francisco, wrote about his attempt to gain a small acting part in a community theatre production. Approximately one hundred people auditioned for the nonpaying role. If you are in a field where the competition is so intense that you have a 1 percent chance of getting a job that pays nothing, then you have to deal with that statistical reality. While having a Plan B would be sensible, I would even suggest that burning your ships in an effort to fully commit to your quixotic endeavor is a reasonable philosophical approach.[7]

Diminished self-esteem from "doing what you love" unsuccessfully is perhaps the most overlooked problem by advisors who urge clients or students to "go for it" without giving much thought to practicality. At some point, lack of practical success affects the psyche, or as one of my clients recently said, "I love my work, but I feel like a failure." Struggling creative clients tell me they grow weary of having conversations about work. They like the part when someone asks them about their artistic endeavors. When the practical questions follow—"How often does your band play?"—they begin to feel inadequate.

---

7 Vikings would burn their ships to prevent retreat when raiding a new territory.

Idealists Need to Be More Practically Skilled Than Realists

Idealists often have to create careers outside the organizational grid. Realists, with the noticeable exception of many business-minded entrepreneurs, often build their careers within structures.

Those working outside the confines of an organization have to worry about such things as managing cash flow, marketing their work, and generating their daily to-do list. Those in traditional full-time jobs do not have such concerns.

Similarly, self-employed idealists have to develop practical skills outside of their expertise. Many people can create beautiful things, but only some can market and sell their things effectively enough to earn a living. Those with traditional full-time jobs need to master their work functions, but not much more.

For these reasons, untethered idealists need to be more concerned about practicality than structure-bound realists.

The Great News about Happy Work

Those who are happy at work, and can at least pay their bills, do not suffer about success in the ways that unhappy workers do. A friend in the financial industry recently said to me, "Everyone has a number," referring to the amount of savings needed to quit or retire. For those who have been battling through tough corporate or other purely practical jobs, this number represents the escape route from a job they don't like. They are like Andy Dufresne in *Shawshank Redemption* building his tunnel through the prison walls, little by little year after year. Financial success for those who don't like their work is reaching that number so they can retire or do something else. Time spent reaching the number uses up an awful lot of life.

For those who are happy in their work, financial numbers are not considered in the same context. Money is not viewed as the key to unlock the work door towards freedom. The happy worker is freely doing what she wants. The iconic image of the old country doctor who still diagnoses townsfolk speaks to this happy reality. Maybe he has to cut his hours, but he won't retire until he can't work anymore. Work is a positive part of his identity. Retirement is viewed as not *being able* to work anymore as opposed to not *having* to work anymore. Those who love their work don't want to retire in the normal sense of the word. They might want to scale back, but why would they want to stop doing what elevates them?

Those who love their work might speak of financial success in terms of paying their bills, funding college for their children, and having enough left over for fun. They talk about retirement in terms of the eventuality of not being able to maintain their full time work energy when elderly. Most idealists then think about how they can still voluntarily contribute to the world. Indeed, when those who love their work crave more money, the desire often emanates from a wish to build their work life to greater heights. More money for those in fulfilling work means a greater capacity to impact the world.

Similarly, yearning for freedom is not an issue for those who are happy at work. In fact, those happily engaged in their careers prefer work to low-quality leisure activities. They feel greater freedom and happiness when working than when attending obligatory social events or so I tell my wife!

Your self-esteem will blossom if you are doing work that stirs your psyche and soul, as you will advance psychologically and spiritually. You feel will good about yourself even if your work is not conventionally prestigious. You will grow to realize what all advanced people do: after a baseline of success is reached, fulfillment and other happiness indicators become more important than superfluous worldly markers.

The best news about happy work is that your career will lead to the transcendence of living life fully in the present. Think about times when you have been immersed in your favorite hobbies. You were not anxious about the future. You were not regretful about the past. You were fully present. That's happy work.

Successful Work

S uccess in the Western world is most commonly construed as financial. Freedom (control of time) and good self-esteem (prestige) are other common markers of success.

Wealth. Money does matter. Some of you will wonder why I'm wasting space stating such an obvious fact. I do so because many young idealists scoff at the importance of money. How do I know? I was one of those scoffers. Taking jobs at nonprofits and government agencies while interviewing at many a public-interest-minded legal organization, "I don't care about money," I said more than a few times. And that was sort of true, as money was simply not high on my list of things that mattered in a job.

Then I had children. For any young idealistic readers, trust me: when you have children, money will matter! At the very least, money can put you in a position to help your family, friends, and good causes.

For everyone else, I know you know.

Your main action step is to gain greater clarity as to how much money you need/desire.

Strategy: Clarifying Financial Success

Financial success would seem to be a quantifiable goal, at least in comparison to other more indefinable goals like good self-esteem. But most have a fuzzy vision of financial success. I have clients ranging from middle class to hedge-fund wealthy, and their views of financial success range similarly: some would feel like they hit the lottery if they earned two hundred thousand dollars, while others would feel impoverished if they earned that same amount.

Strategy: Gaining Clarity on Financial Success
Generate three numbers:

After-tax income to maintain your current lifestyle
If you don't know this number, you are far from alone. It's the first number needed so that you can plan what you need to cut if forced, and so you can determine what is needed for your transition.

After-tax income to meet your basic needs
The basics are food, shelter (including utilities), and clothing. In industrial societies, the basics also include insurance, transportation, and communication. After meeting the basics in these categories, you are moving into the range of lifestyle preferences that are beyond necessity.

We live well by most every standard of living in the history of humankind, so areas of fat within your current lifestyle can likely be identified. The challenge for most of us is identifying what constitutes basic needs. I ask my clients to pretend they are time-travelers from the Great Depression era. What would that person say was needed? Some mode of transportation? Yes. A luxury car? No.

After-tax income to obtain your future lifestyle goals
I don't mean "all your wildest dreams." Indeed, it seems clear that much of societal unhappiness stems from excessive material wants. While this list could include some desired toys, idealistic aspirations are more likely to include travelling, helping your aging parents, or saving for your children's college tuition.

With these numbers in place, you can better plan which career track can meet your financial needs for success.

Financial Risk for Happiness
When I counsel clients on potential entrepreneurial ventures, their fear of financial ruin is almost always present. Surprisingly, despite news of our collective lack of financial responsibility, I have met far more overly cautious clients than those who plunged recklessly into ill-advised ventures. I recognize the likelihood that the type of people who do the latter don't take the time to consult with career counselors.

Nonetheless, far more of my clients overestimate the probability of financial calamities. For example, Kathy was contemplating scaling back her work at a coffeehouse to start a service business that required minimal capital investment. The business was her dream. She had several clients already and had good leads on many more. Those initial clients had committed to buying Kathy's services sufficient to produce approximately one thousand dollars a month in profit for the next three months. She had never done the math, but she knew that she spent more than that per month and had decided against going forward.

After Kathy did her homework and came back with her three financial numbers, she felt much better about taking the plunge. She needed about two thousand dollars a month for a bare minimum lifestyle by her standards; about twenty-five hundred dollars a month to maintain her current lifestyle; and about three thousand dollars a month for her desired lifestyle, which would include luxuries such as travel and attending concerts. She had twenty-seven thousand dollars in savings. Moreover, she did not have to quit her coffeehouse job; the manager would let her work part time, generating roughly one thousand dollars a month in income.

As we dispassionately went through the analysis, Kathy realized that at the very least, the combination of her initial clients plus her part-time work would enable her to maintain her basic lifestyle without dipping into savings.[8] Thereafter, even if her current clients did not continue and no new clients came in—a worst-case scenario—she would not be financially ruined. She would be out some money but nothing cataclysmic would have occurred. Moreover, it was likely she could go back to working full time at the coffeehouse and then either move on knowing that she had tried or regroup for a second attempt.

But what if the business did succeed? Her whole life would change for the better. She would go to work happy and she would be successful. Some risks are worth it.

Freedom. While wealth might be the most discernable success factor, freedom—control over your own time—is a goal that seems to be growing in importance throughout our culture.

---

8 She also could use credit cards or credit lines. These really do provide a cash flow back stop, and many successful entrepreneurs launched their businesses fueled by credit. Still, since so many people use credit irresponsibly, I rarely advocate such use.

The 4-Hour Workweek, by Tim Ferriss, is the most well-known book that captures the philosophy of working as a means to generate freedom. If you haven't read the book, you should—Ferriss is insightful and hilarious. Although he knowingly exaggerates, he was touching on the notion that there is a better way to spend one's work life than grinding out fifty- to sixty-hour work weeks year after year in the hopes of creating enough wealth to enjoy life thirty to forty years down the road.[9]

For Ferriss, the creation of passive income—income generated without the need for much effort—is the foundation for creating freedom. He advocates building passive income-generating systems that enable as much freedom as possible. For most, this would mean creating or being part of some type of entrepreneurial venture. It also could mean that you discover how to maximize flexibility within an organizational structure. Ferriss is not fully in touch with the realities of building such systems. He did, so he thinks everyone can, but not everyone is a superenergetic, autodidactic polymath like Ferriss. Moreover, successfully building passive income systems takes talent and many hours. The footnote to his *4-Hour* title should be that several years of forty-plus hours a week are required to be in position to live a four-hour work week. Nonetheless, he struck a huge chord with readers eager to seek an alternative to the "work hard for forty years so you can have fun in retirement" mentality.

I recall one of my career epiphanies when I was a young attorney in Washington, DC. My friend was working on

---

9 Ferriss worked far more than four hours a week to launch his business, and works far more than that now. He realizes the reader knows this and seems to be mischievously winking as he writes.

a trial with famed lawyer Brendan Sullivan (perhaps his most well-known individual client was Lieutenant-Colonel Oliver North). Sullivan was among the most respected litigators in the country. He was in his fifties at the time and had already more than paid his dues and made his mark. Nonetheless, he worked alongside my young attorney friend from seven in the morning to nine at night for nearly three months to work a trial held in Cleveland. Sullivan is a master of his craft and, I assume, enjoys his work. It was a revelation to me, however, as I realized that even if I worked incredibly hard for a couple of decades, I would still have to put in fourteen-hour days and be away from my family. And unlike Sullivan, I didn't enjoy litigation that much.

Ferriss had a similar epiphany when he saw what he describes as an old, fat, bald guy in a BMW convertible. He wondered how long it took for that man to be in position to finally enjoy life. Almost immediately thereafter, Ferriss left his corporate job to build a highly successful online nutritional supplements company. Unlike most entrepreneurs, his goal was not to keep building the company to maximize wealth. Instead, he wanted to build it sufficiently enough to maximize freedom. It's worth mentioning that Ferriss does not equate freedom with sitting around doing nothing—he passionately indulges in his various hobbies.

A subculture of this freedom trend even more radically incorporates freedom as part of the Path of Abundance. Chris Guillebeau's book, *The $100 Startup*, perhaps best illustrates this idea. Guillebeau and his peers are not out to create the next Microsoft, but rather the next microbusiness that will provide the freedom to live and work anywhere.

Guillebeau created a one-person company based on his own travel experience. Having set a personal goal to visit every country in the world, but not having the funds to do so, Guillebeau became a master at navigating frequent flyer rules. He wrote and self-published a how-to guide on the subject, developed Internet marketing skills to sell the guide, and created a small business around this travel niche, later adding other areas of expertise. Given his desire for freedom to travel, he has no interest in creating a larger company with time-draining and location-fixing management and operations responsibilities. His book documents the formula for success of other fellow microbusiness owners: develop an expertise related to a product or a service that does not require one's physical presence; learn how to market it effectively; make the process repeatable; and relish in genuine freedom.

These entrepreneurs illustrate that freedom—as much as wealth—is a part of the Path of Abundance. The counterexample also makes the point: I routinely hear someone cut down an otherwise successful worker by noting, "Sure, he has a big job, but he has no life."[10]

Strategy: How Can You Earn Money Without Being at a Workplace?

Brainstorm what income you can create that would not require your physical presence. This could include telecommuting for large organizations. What passive streams of income can you generate? Income from rental properties, sales from products on your website, and royalties from creative works are examples. Each requires investment of

10 Kevin Roose's great book, *Young Money*, about Wall Street investment banking analysts, provides keen insight on this dichotomy.

time and energy to establish but, postcreation, will become the foundation for securing your freedom. For the talented, the New World of Work really can be virtual. Each year, I speak to an increasing number of entrepreneurs with a home office as their primary work place. Even better, the home office is now the portable office since a laptop, phone, and Internet connection are all that is needed for many knowledge-economy workers. I teach several law and government online classes. Years back, I was worried that an overseas vacation during one of the semesters would be looked at dimly by the university administration even though I would have Internet access while away. Instead, the response was quite the opposite: "Post pictures! What a great advertisement to our students about the benefits of online education and a great recruiting tool for hiring other professors!"

Self-esteem. How do you feel about yourself based on your occupation? Perhaps it should not be so, but our jobs have a significant effect on our identities. This explains why Supreme Court justices will work for pay that is not much more than what young attorneys in big-city firms earn, and why my suggestion to some young clients that they should consider plumbing (a high-paying, secure field) is usually met with immediate dismissal.

Self-esteem, or at least your need for public approval, might pose an initial challenge on your Path of Abundance. Doing something idealistic usually means doing something unconventional. If you choose to do something that is different than most, you may find yourself worried about what the rest of that herd thinks of you. While a course of action that leads to happy and successful work need not be unconventional, the New World of Work calls for unconventional thinking.

In the Old World of Work, gaining entry into a Fortune 500 company, playing corporate warrior, and battling into an executive position was the conventional path to success (but not necessarily happiness). Working as a doctor, lawyer, or within other professions was the alternate standard route. While mavericks and the well-capitalized might have chosen the entrepreneurial path, most people did not choose to work outside the organizational world. For those who did, prestige came only if the company or unusual career was built successfully. When Steve Jobs started Apple, he would have been dismissed as just another hippie by the conventional 1970s corporate man. Fortunately, he didn't care. People who cared what the undefined general masses would think had to muster great courage to pursue a dream.

While the entrepreneurial path—be it literally as an entrepreneur or simply as someone on an unusual career course—is far more accepted today, even lauded in certain circles, you will still have to brave some odd looks if you do something out of the ordinary.

Strategy: Reconfigure the Standard Definition of Status

I recall a funny career story told to me by a legal recruiter named Leslie. She suffered through years of work as an associate at a big Boston law firm with the goal of becoming a partner. She came from an affluent family, so while the elevated income was an added benefit, it was not her major goal. Leslie had been a status striver all her life, but had never been happy. She thought becoming a partner would make her happy. It didn't. After being named partner—the end goal of her eight years of suffering—she quit almost immediately.

Leslie realized that she given up an enormous amount of her life for the sake of conventional prestige. She decided not to let the rest of her life be dictated by concerns about what others might think.

I use the phrase "off the grid" when I talk about people who have moved away from traditional corporate structures. Those who start entrepreneurial ventures or otherwise move into arenas without organizational charts almost always realize how silly it was to attach self-esteem to something as arbitrary as a title.

"My career goal is to become a vice-president in the company," Kathleen said.

"But you just said you hate working in your company," I replied.

"I know but I see the respect vice-presidents get from everyone."

"*Everyone?* You mean a few dozen people in your company."

I explained to Kathleen that she was so immersed in her company's culture that she had confused "everyone" with her colleagues in her corporate office. Most people in an organizational machine don't realize they are living in a provincial microcosm that uses a person's job title to convey status—anthropologically the same as certain status symbols in a primitive village. Those off the grid don't care about your title.

Think through your prestige needs. Separate career goals authentic to you—you might genuinely want a leadership position and thereby need to have a title that gives you authority—from inauthentic goals designed to impress others. You might find that you are wasting a lot of time and energy on inauthentic needs.

Phase III: Go

Career Frameworks

Psychological Blocks

Transactional vs. Opportunity Cost

Situational Analysis

Career Frameworking

meet most of our clients after they have made some type of career commitment. This ranges from those who are in the midst of a thirty-year career to those who have committed to a college major. For those who are unhappy in their choice, I need to shift the view that they are trapped. The unhappily employed almost always overinflate the importance of their present occupation; their suffering stems from overidentifying with their job. Idealists are more prone to this challenge than others because they expect their work to be meaningful and an extension of their inner selves.

Viewing your work within the context of an overall plan makes a happiness difference because the "why" of what you are doing matters profoundly. Parents changing diapers and working two jobs know their "why." Graduate students, actors, and bootstrap entrepreneurs working menial jobs similarly understand the "why." Those without the "why" face existential crises.

Why Does "Why" Matter So Much?
The Constructs of Identity and Permanency
If you don't understand why you are working in a dismal job, your psychological and cultural programming related to identity and permanency takes hold. When high-school students work summer jobs in fast-food establishments, they

derive neither a sense of identity nor permanency from their jobs. They are working for money. That's it. But when twenty-something college graduates work at the same exact burger joints, many develop psychological angst related to their job identities. Their self-esteem suffers. In addition, since there is no distinct end in sight—like the end of the summer for the student—the indefinite future translates into a sense of permanency. Despondency results because they have not properly framed their job as simply work that pays the bills.

Understanding why you are doing something will invariably make your work life better. Frameworks defining what work you are doing will help. While it may seem a matter of semantics, if you are employed doing something that you don't like, replace "job" with "work" and then delineate your work as follows:

McDonald's Work: Work that pays the bills but is not part of your big-picture plan, does not represent your identity, and is not envisioned as permanent.

Exploratory Work: Work that helps you find your desired career field. This is usually unpaid work such as all the actions you take to evaluate potential fields of interest. This is the work that is most needed.

Pay-Your-Dues Work: Work that is necessary to achieve the work you really want to do. You have to go to medical school if you want to be a doctor. You have to take an entry-level job to get to management. You have to learn coding before writing an app.

McDonald's Work

I emphasize that all work—at least that which is not immoral—has honor. Nothing about the term McDonald's

Work is meant to denigrate any type of job. If I had to dig ditches to support my family, then that's what I would do without any compunction that such work was beneath me. Moreover, I would do it as best as possible. So, if you are stuck in work that you don't like but need to pay your bills, feel grateful that you have such work and do the best job you can while you plot your next move.

Actors who wait tables best illustrate this framework. By economic definition, based on both the percentage of hours worked and money earned, most are full-time waiters who have sporadic part-time acting gigs. Nonetheless, ask a waiter-actress what she does for a living, and she will respond, "I am an actress."

McDonald's Work pays the bills. Since you need to pay the bills, be happy for its place within your career plan, but don't overidentify with such jobs. We have shopping outlets near our offices that are wonderful job providers for college students who happily work such jobs. But upon graduating, they become highly anxious if they have not found a career-building job. With one such client, I pointed out that she had now internalized the job as part of her identity. She had shifted from "I work at the mall" to "I am a mall worker." Idealists particularly suffer with identity issues because their job selling high-priced jeans is not part of who they are.

Overidentification with your current job will cause unhappiness if you do not frame it as a "pay the bills" job. While McDonald's Work could literally be slinging fries, such work does not necessarily mean low pay and low prestige. Many business executives would lump their six-figure salary vice-presidencies within this category. They hate their jobs. In their cases, identity is not really an issue so much as permanency. A large part of their distress stems from feeling that they are locked into their jobs for-ever. When my clients understand that their current jobs will end soon enough, they feel palpably relieved. They understand that their current work is paying the bills, but their identity will be more aligned with their next venture.

The McDonald's Work framework might not make your work day go much easier. You might still grumble when serving an ungrateful customer more coffee. If you know your work is just to make money and only for a distinct pe-riod of time, however, then your nights will go easier, as you won't suffer over issues of identity and permanency. If you are taking classes in web design, but paying your bills otherwise, mentally restructure how you view your work. "I am becoming a web designer. I work at Starbucks to help pay the bills." You will feel better about yourself and about your job at the coffee shop.

Exploratory Work

If you are wondering what you should do now, the an-swer is spend meaningful time and energy engaged in Exploratory Work. Developing Intrapersonal and Entrepreneurial Wisdom is the end goal; Exploratory Work is the road to reach it.

Most people drift into their careers. Structured and meaningful career exploration is not a part of the school system. As such, you are responsible for creating your own career exploration projects. This is the work that not only will help you choose your career path, but that answers "why" you are doing your McDonald's and Pay-Your-Dues work to get on your path.

Exploratory Work leads to answers to "Why am I doing this?" Without reflection, most suffer in jobs that they have deemed meaningless. More significantly, they won't put in the time necessary to develop their skills to move toward a better path. If your Exploratory Work enables you to craft a plan that calls for working as an office temp (Pay-Your-Bills Work) while taking night classes in a field of interest (Pay-Your-Dues Work), then you will understand the meaning of your daily grind. Those who feel purposeful even in the midst of drudgery go to bed feeling satisfied.

Why Exploratory Work Provides a Critical Advantage for Your Job/Career Search

Exploratory Work provides focus. Those on the job/career hunt using a targeted rifle are at a serious advantage compared to those using the scattered shotgun approach. Looking for anything and everything usually leads to nothing.

When you discover what you want, not only will you be able to precisely tell others your objective, which helps others help you, but your reticular activating system (RAS) will alert you to possibilities that lead to your goal. The RAS is your brain's search engine: it filters out extraneous details in our overloaded information world and, more importantly, will help you focus attention on what you want.

How does this work? Once your Exploratory Work leads to a distinct interest in a certain industry, all news items, conversations, and thoughts related to that sector will seem to magically appear. Those triggers were always present. Previously, you had filtered *out* instead of filtering *in* this information. Optimizing your RAS by deciding what to focus upon will maximize your energy both in a literal and abstract sense. Concentrating on distinct opportunities within a potential career field will yield better results than scanning online job boards for something that might fit.

Moreover, if you know what you want, you will be more effective in telling others who are in a position to help you. It is very hard to help people who want "a job." I have edited many resumes with vaguely stated objectives such as "a challenging job that is suited to my skills." If anything, this phrase tips off the reader that you don't know what you want. It is far easier to help someone who wants "a marketing position in the biotech sector in New Haven."

Creating Your Own Exploratory Work Structure

What is exploratory career work? Reading this book is one example. Exploratory Work could be viewed as everything you do to chart your career path prior to actual work in your field of interest. The lack of opportunity for meaningful career exploration may be the biggest failing of our education system; therefore, creating your own Exploratory Work may be your secret weapon for career success.

Reflecting on your vision while going for a long walk, talking to a business-savvy friend, and reading up on different industries are among the myriad of simple exploratory tasks that can be done at any time. Informational interviewing, job shadowing, meeting with a career counselor, volunteering, and interning are more formal possibilities.

As you read the above, you might have pondered why your high school and college did not provide enough similar opportunities. Most young adults have a minimal understanding of different career options, but feel compelled to commit to a specific career without having anywhere near sufficient information to make such a life-changing decision. Wouldn't it make sense if recent graduates were provided a structure to read up on different career paths, talk to those who are in their fields of interest, choose several that seem the most promising fit, and then rotate through a one- or two-week-long job-shadowing program? That does not happen and is not going to happen anytime soon.

So you have to design your own Exploratory Work. Creating a distinct work structure as you would with any work project is your first step. Here you are likely to grapple with the emotional more than the practical challenges of Exploratory Work.

My client Elaine was a lawyer who spent much of her day researching case law. When I assigned her research for career exploration, I could immediately sense her stress. She agreed to do the work, but noted that as soon as she started researching her career options, her anxiety would kick in. As will be discussed in the forthcoming section on psychological blocks, she had to learn to be dispassionate when engaged in research. In Elaine's case, I asked her to pretend the research was for me. That eased her mind.

As it is with most learning, your initial work should involve some combination of research, reading, and reflection. Thereafter, have discussions with people in fields of interest, wise people in your life who know you well, and perhaps, respected career counselors. Finally, if possible, tangibly explore fields of interest through informational interviews, job shadowing, volunteering, and interning.

If you are able to secure a part-time job in your field of interest, then you will have discovered the goldmine of Exploratory Work and really the first step of Pay-Your-Dues Work.

Types of Transformation to Explore: Rejuvenation, Relaunching, and Reinvention

Unless you are just starting out and *choosing* your career, Exploratory Work will lead you to *transform* your career. Here are the major types of transformations that you can make:

Rejuvenation: Staying In Your Job/Career Path But Reconfiguring The Way You Work.

If your job is making you miserable, I imagine that resistance is emerging right now, perhaps for good reason. It is likely that you are reading this book because there is no simple fix for your current career challenge. You might be thinking, "If I could make my current work situation better, I would." Still, rejuvenation should be considered—it involves the least amount of disruption.

Upward Linear: The Most Common Form of Rejuvenation

If you are working in an organization, analyze whether you would like a direct upward promotion within the same or similar organization. Historically, promotions were far and away the most common form of career rejuvenation. Moving up the ladder provided automatic revitalization for many. It still might for you.

But be cautious—you might be tempted to view the promotion only in comparison to your current job. Presumably, the job above yours has a better salary, greater autonomy, and more interesting responsibilities.

You would likely take that job over your current job if those were the only two options, but that's not the proper analysis.

Instead, compare jobs in other career paths. That examination would focus on whether it is worth putting in more time in your current job. Since your current job is most directly leading you to potentially moving upward in linear fashion, more time at your current job is costing you time that could be spent in a better-suited field.

Analyzing your upward linear move is crucial for career considerations. If you don't want the promotion to your next job, staying put makes no sense unless you want to stay in your current job in perpetuity.

One of the first things I ask new clients who work in organizations is, "Would you want your boss's job?" Benjamin, a midlevel executive at a pharmaceutical company, heard that question and blurted out, "No way!" He then looked at me and said, "I get it. I have to go."

Shifting Critical Components of Your Job

There are other ways to rejuvenate your current job. Can you switch your work unit to escape a terrible boss or unlikable coworkers? Can you develop a new skill within the contours of your job? Create a new client base? Work from home?

I recently worked with Jim, a midcareer service professional who had grown weary of the day-to-day dullness of his job. He didn't dislike his work. Instead, he wondered whether any other career path might interest him.

Jim's learning curve had flattened—twenty years of working within one field will do that—and his income had plateaued.

He noted, as have many clients, that the increase in pay during the first few years on the job made him feel better about his pay then than he does now, even though he is making more money. We feel good when are progressing, so Jim now felt like he was in a rut.

After analyzing Jim's financial and life situation, two things were clear: (1) he would have really high transactional costs to switch fields, as he was currently earning a high income; and (2) there was really nothing else in particular he was interested in doing—he was just fishing for options.

When we discussed the most interesting cutting-edge area of service within his field, Jim became animated in conversation. Initially, he had been reluctant to invest time and energy in a new area. I then pointed out that rejuvenation is as much of a mental attitude as it is a series of practical tasks. He could think about his potential new service area while commuting, getting ready for work, or doing his chores. Since this area was genuinely exciting to him, such thinking would be energy enhancing rather than draining. Jim left smiling and seemingly immersed in thought about his new area of interest.

Relaunching: Staying Within The Same Field But Switching Work Platforms.
The Lateral Move: The Most Common Form of Relaunching

If you like your work but don't like your organization, then this move makes sense: you could move sideways to a different organization in the same industry and maintain the same general job. Before doing so, however, your analysis should center upon whether your company is really much different from other companies in the industry.

I observed many big-city law associates leap from one large law firm to another in a triumph of hope over logic. Unless they had switched from a particularly horrible partner at the old firm to a particularly kind partner at the new one, they soon discovered that more of the same awaited them. Will the same basic hierarchical structure, pressures, and personalities await you at a new company in the same industry? If so, the lateral move is not likely your panacea.

There are other types of lateral moves:

Same Industry, Different Function

Some successful paths involve blending skills within the same industry or organization. Jack Welch started as an engineer before he moved to the business side of General Electric. Many scientists in the pharmaceutical world make similar moves to business functions within the pharmaceutical industry. Here you would have to be convinced that you really like your industry, but have reasons to move into a different functional area.

Same Function, Different Industry

Taking your functional expertise and moving into a different industry is another common move. You may enjoy sales but have tired of selling insurance products. You could stay in sales and move into the high-tech industry. For this type of move, you need to be convinced that you like your function but would prosper in a different industry.

Advanced Training

Getting more training is another way of relaunching one's career. This includes learning new skills and gaining new credentials. Graduate school is the most common form of advanced training.

I had the pleasure of working with Donna, a young, successful entrepreneur who had opened a retail store in deep suburbia. The store was a success, and she had been happy while she was building that success. Now she was on autopilot and stuck in a place where her social life was limited.

On a professional level, Donna realized that she loved the marketing aspect of building her business, but the operational aspect bored her. She decided that she would prefer working in a big city for a larger company in her industry— her success as an entrepreneur might make her an interesting job candidate for an innovative company. Generally speaking, however, most corporations avoid hiring entrepreneurs. By definition, entrepreneurs do not fit large corporate culture. Donna discovered this to be true and came back in a funk: "Am I stuck working in my shop forever?"

Donna's business success made her an excellent candidate for an MBA program, particularly as a young female entrepreneur. Post-MBA, Donna would likely have her pick of jobs at those big-city fashion companies. In addition, Donna would have other options in the world of possibilities an elite business school would provide. At the time of this writing, Donna was relaunching, armed with an elite business school's resources.

Reinvention: Go To an Entirely Different Career Path.

Reinvention involves dramatic change. It is the "out of the box" option and often the romantic dream of idealists.

Doing something different, chasing the dream, and starting a new venture are all highly attractive.

Those who are unemployed, underemployed, or unhappily fully employed but have no idea what to do for their career, usually need to reinvent themselves. Why did you pick up this book? If you are like most of my clients, you are seeking something "out of the box."

From college students who enter my office, I usually hear: "I am majoring in 'X,' but I have no idea what I want to do."

From twentysomethings with jobs: "I don't know what I want to do, but I know I don't want to be doing this."

From thirty and fortysomethings: "What else can I do with my background?"

From fiftysomethings: "I need to work for another ten to twenty years and I think I owe it to myself and my legacy to find work that I would actually like doing."

Out-of-the-box moves are the most challenging because we are cultured in a lock step society that compels obligatory moves from one step to the next: first grade to second grade and so forth. The Old World of Work had a similar feel, as organizational charts set the structure for one's career. The out-of-the-box move is at once liberating and dizzying. It is wonderful that you can choose to do anything, yet challenging to create from a blank slate. Regardless, when reinvention works it is beautiful to behold.

I went to the same law school as Gerald Levin. He's thirty years older than I am, but through the alumni news I saw the last part of his career unfold. If Levin's name sounds vaguely familiar, it is because he was the CEO of Time Warner, and later AOL Time Warner. Outside of Bill Gates and a few others, Levin was the most powerful corporate executive in the world for a brief time.

Then it all came crashing down. The merger that Levin shepherded between AOL and Time Warner is now considered among the worst business moves in corporate history, and it led to his ouster in 2001. That's the last I heard of Levin until I read an article about him in *The New Yorker* in 2007.

Levin was now running Moonview Sanctuary, a holistic healing institute. The entire interview could have been a case study on the transformation of an unhappy success—as he described his time in the corporate world—to a happy success. While he was no longer earning multimillions, the institute was doing very well by normal standards, and he was beyond happy.

Levin's transformation, while extreme, illustrates the possibilities of reinvention. My own story, while far less dramatic, does so as well and demonstrates the increasing normalcy of reinvention in the New World of Work. When I transitioned in the early 2000s from attorney to education entrepreneur, I had to endure many polite, and some not-so-polite, versions of "Why would you do such a thing?" That I was "following my calling as an educator" was the most authentic answer. Knowing that such a response created odd looks, particularly from the conventional set, I would more often focus on the entrepreneur part.

Now, perhaps because of the tumultuous forces of change in the last decade, the switch has flipped. I get far more questions about "how" I was able to move into work that I had a calling for. More people nowadays seem to intuitively understand the "why."

Pay-Your-Dues Work

Most fields require that you pay your dues. While it is disheartening that so many people get depressed when they inflate the identification of their McDonald's Work, it is even worse that many people will not venture into fields that seem to suit them because they feel the Pay-Your-Dues Work will affect their identity. Idealists seem to have particular challenges with paying their dues: the quest for the ideal makes anything on the lower level of the path less than ideal.

I have had clients express utter dismay in their current career path. They believed the new career path that we discussed held far better promise for their future happiness and success, but would balk at venturing onto that path when they realized they would have to take a step down in pay or prestige. I understand the feeling. Taking one step backward—even if you know it will lead to two steps forward—is difficult in the short run. But like anything worthwhile, investment—Pay-Your-Dues Work—is necessary if you want to follow a new path. Those stories of CEOs who started in the mail room were about enterprising young adults who long ago paid their dues.

The most common form of Pay-Your-Dues Work is graduate school. Given the costs of higher education, I want to ensure my clients are committed to their chosen path before making such an investment. But credentials and training are essential for some fields, and you can't become a doctor or lawyer without paying for and attending medical or law school. Similarly, for those interested in honing their skills or building their credentials, degrees, certifications, and classes will matter. You want to create a great app that helps save the planet by making consumers aware of their environmental footprint? You had better invest in learning how to code or get credentials sufficient to be hired by an app maker.

Pay-Your-Dues Work is important not only to help categorize work in your mind, but to develop the skills and knowledge that will ensure the success of your venture. For example, many people dream of starting a restaurant: they picture being proud restaurant owners in a beautiful establishment with attractive wait staff leading happy customers to their tables. They envision hiring top chefs, reading rave reviews, and greeting impressed guests.

Restaurants fail regularly because most new owners have not paid their dues adequately. If they had, they would likely have discovered that chefs tend to be temperamental; ordering the best ingredients is expensive; and dealing with complaints is far more common than accepting compliments. So if you want to start a restaurant and have never worked in one before, you should not be above waiting tables, bussing dishes, or any other restaurant job that will teach you how to operate a restaurant and deal with those crazy chefs.

Path-of-Abundance Work

That's why you are reading this book. You want work that is on your chosen career path. Getting on your path doesn't mean that your work world will be perfect. You likely will be paying your dues while getting a toehold on the first part of your path. But when you know you are on your path, work life is glorious.

How Does This Work in Real Life?

Mike, age twenty-seven, came in to see me because he felt stifled in his job. He was working as a business development associate in the tech industry. "I'm in a tough spot. I'm in business development, basically sales, for my company. If I don't bring in business, I'll be fired. I think our products are OK, but not that great. If I'm fired at sales, it will look like I can't sell. I don't know what I should do. Should I go back to school? Get an MBA? Get a computer technology degree? Or should I just go do something else. Maybe financial sales?"

Mike mentioned financial sales because he wanted to have greater control of his destiny. While he definitely wanted to make more money, he also had a psychological urge to have his success linked more directly to his abilities.

An out-of-the-box move did not really make sense. Mike liked his industry. His interest in considering a computer tech degree stemmed from his genuine fascination with technology. He noted that he wasn't a "geek," so he had never been into computers or coding in high school. Still, he really loved high tech, and at least for a nontechie, was quite savvy. The upward linear path also did not make much sense because Mike would simply have a higher job in sales for a company whose products he didn't really like.

Mike had an idea for an app that he believed had real commercial viability. He worried that if he told his company, he would either be ignored or the idea would be stolen. Regardless, he couldn't capitalize on his idea because he needed tech skills to make it a reality. Given what he wanted to do, an MBA was not required—for entry to some parts of big business, MBAs are essential. Graduate schools provide a platform for people to relaunch, figure out new paths, and reinvent after experiencing the spark of connection with other smart people. MBAs are sometimes critical to future success. MBAs can also cost one hundred thousand dollars, which Mike would have to fund himself.

As for a computer tech degree, Mike did not want to become a full-time techie; he just wanted sufficient skills so that he could develop the prototype of his own app and be knowledgeable enough to direct a staff. When we first met, I suggested that he start with free coding lessons from online entities. He did, and thought the time was valuable.

A few months later, an opportunity came. One of the tech guys at his company was starting his own venture and wanted Mike to be on the sales team. Mike asked if he could also help with coding, but his friend said no because Mike was not yet up to speed.

I suggested that Mike ask if he could help with tech stuff for free. In Old World of Work thinking, working for free would seem crazy. In New World of Work thinking, Mike would be getting trained in a critical skill and get real hands-on tech experience.

They worked out a deal: Mike would spend approximately thirty hours on sales and ten hours on technical work each week. The catch was that he would not be paid for his technical work, and his sales salary would be low. Unless his commissions were really high, he would not be able to pay all his bills.

Mike needed some McDonald's Work. He had another friend who helped get him a job bartending on Saturday nights. It wasn't bad, because it was a social job. He got to meet young women and work with his friend—not bad for McDonald's work, he told me. He was continuing his Exploratory Work by honing his app idea and taking an online coding class through Code Academy. His new job was a combination of Pay-Your-Dues and Path-of-Abundance Work. His next step will be to develop his app for his new company, take it to another company, or start a company on his own.

Psychological Blocks to Career Success

As you get your plan in place, you must get over your inner obstacles. Here are some common psychological blocks:

The Perils of Choice

"You can grow up and do whatever you want." That's what our elders told us. Our freedom to choose, while brilliant in theory, has also created enormous challenges. As Barry Schwartz pointed out in *The Paradox of Choice*, vast possibilities create their own set of problems. In relation to career choice, parents tell their children they can grow up to do whatever they want. It's a nice sentiment, and I don't discourage parents from conveying this thought to young children. Nonetheless, when young adults tell me that they are lost in part because of seemingly endless career possibilities, I know that the open-ended nature of choice is part of the problem.

Think back a couple of generations. Imagine you were the son or daughter of a farmer in Iowa. Unless you were quite adventurous, you knew your future. You were going to be an Iowa farmer or an Iowa farmer's wife (along with all the farm and house work that she would do). That may sound dim to many. Variety is generally a good thing.

Career choice variety, however, can also be headache inducing.[11]

Moreover, career difficulties are dissimilar to math problems. You can't sit down with a pen and paper and figure out that you should become an account executive at an advertising agency. Analytical intelligence can get someone only so far in a framework that lacks certainty.

Entrepreneurial Wisdom—your ability to navigate the outer world—will help you understand which of these roads make sense to explore. This will help you quickly sort out the real from the imagined. In the same way that you ruled out professional athlete or pop star, you will narrow your choices based on real-world sensibility.

Your Intrapersonal Wisdom will lead you to the realization that the attractive but maddeningly open-ended "I can do anything" should be replaced by the wiser "These are the fields I should tangibly explore."

Strategy: Option Analysis
What are your real options? Ten-year-olds think they can simultaneously become Oscar-winning actors and Olympic gymnasts. No need to disillusion them. But twenty-, thirty- and even forty-year-olds engage in a similar strand of thinking: "There are so many things I want to do!" To provide clarity, I walk clients through their real options. Depending on their age and credentials, we often wind up with only two or three real options to pursue. Unquestionably, there are numerous iterations within the

---

11 I remember anxiously mulling over a mere two job offers with similar parameters in terms of location, type of work, and salary. I discussed my dilemma with a wise elder. He responded, "You want to give a man a bellyache? Offer him two jobs." He was right.

options—you can head into marketing by taking an entry-level job at Cartoon Network in Atlanta, or by joining a three-person marketing team in Darien, Connecticut focused on marketing for financial professionals.

By heading toward one real field, you will position yourself to reap the rewards of cultivating a single tree as opposed to dreaming of, but never building, a forest.

"It Will Come to Me"

You might have thought, "It will come to me." Why? Did your parents or some well-meaning adult tell you that over time you would figure out what to do with your career? There is a pervasive cultural myth that sometime during high school or college we would figure out what work we wanted to do for the rest of our lives. How this actually happens is never quite explained.

At most, young adults are told that they will take classes in something they like that will lead to natural gravitation toward a specific career. The mismatch between high-school classes and real-world careers, while never particularly correlative, has grown increasingly wider. As for college, the challenges facing liberal-arts students choosing careers are now well known. I loved my philosophy, theology, psychology, English, government, and history classes. The education itself was enlightening, enriching, and stimulating. Indeed, the Great Books are often source material for developing Intrapersonal Wisdom. I struggle to say anything negative about a liberal-arts education. However, the course work provided minimal career insight.

As for business students, most are doing course work that more closely provides exposure to career choice.

Nevertheless, there are radical variations in business careers. Creating Excel spreadsheets from reams of statistical data is a business job, but so is creating a multimedia marketing campaign.

Engineers, premeds, and others in technical fields are far closer to getting simultaneous academic and career training. The problem is that the course work itself does not compel students to sort out big-picture career questions. The eighteen-year-old college freshman who chose her specialist technical path correctly has good fortune. Those who chose incorrectly become unhappy thirtysomething doctors and computer programmers.

Intrapersonal Wisdom will compel you to discipline yourself to do necessary career exploration rather than engage in magical thinking that "it will come to me." Entrepreneurial Wisdom will lead you to put a process into place so that you can tangibly evaluate different fields.

Strategy: Set Aside Time Each Week to Actively Engage in Exploratory Work

Design your own career course. Or take a career development course. At the very least, put some structure into your quest.

Ellen explained her day. She worked from nine in the morning to six at night, and after work she went out with friends, took an aerobics class, cooked dinner, read a book, or watched TV. On the weekends, she would travel to see her boyfriend, or he would visit her. This sounds fine and would have been if she had not been completely miserable in her job for the last six years. Her Exploratory Work consisted of applying to random jobs that she would periodically see on online job boards. She spent no real concentrated time deciphering what to do when she grew up. She came to see me because she realized she actually was grown up and had to actively engage in figuring out her career because "It might never come to me."

Analysis Paralysis and Dealing with Ambiguity
Perhaps more than any other block, analysis paralysis blocks people from moving forward: those frozen in career blocks are often stuck because of process and outcome ambiguity. I am not referring to the feeling of being lost—having no idea what to do is different than knowing the right direction but being unable to move forward. Clients can't move forward because they do not know how to move forward (process ambiguity) and/or because the results of moving forward are not guaranteed (outcome ambiguity). Use Entrepreneurial Wisdom to address process ambiguity, and Intrapersonal Wisdom to address outcome ambiguity.

Process Ambiguity
"I have no idea what graduate programs would help me."
"How will I get the money to start a business?"
"I don't know how I will be able to make a career switch."

These are process issues that have practical answers. You might not like some of those answers. Within reason, however, process issues can be sorted out.

Strategy: Work-Arounds Solve Most Process Issues
Process issues usually have practical solutions that I call work-arounds: if you are committed to getting around

a tangible problem, there is most often a strategic way around, over, or through the problem or at least a way to deal with the challenge well enough to move forward.

"You can spend a few hours researching graduate programs that might suit you."

"You can wait tables while you start your business."

"Find someone who switched fields from your current one to another. Buy her lunch and listen to her story."

Most work-arounds are not perfect. Presumably, you would rather hang out with your friends on Saturday night than wait tables, and would feel awkward asking a stranger to tell her story. I never said getting on the Path of Abundance would be easy.

"I don't know how to create a website," Gail said. This was one of ten different objections Gail had to launching a side business. "If I demonstrate that you can build a website, will you then realize that your other objections are equally solvable?" I proposed.

As those of you who have used simple site-building software know, building a basic website is surprisingly easy. Gail was stunned by the simplicity, and agreed that she would now look at process challenges differently.

Outcome Ambiguity

Unlike process ambiguity, which has answers for what can be done, outcome ambiguity exists because there are no real answers, just reasonable predictions to "what if" questions.

"What if I don't get admitted?"

"What if I don't get hired?"

"What if the business makes no money?"

Strategy: The Dispassionate Scientist Exercise

Outcome ambiguity cannot be solved like process ambiguity. You can research schools, search for jobs, and start writing a business plan, and each of these activities relieves the anxiety that comes from process ambiguity. The anxiety stemming from outcome ambiguity is fundamentally different because uncertainty about the outcome is the only thing guaranteed as you move forward. The best you can do is remove emotion as you evaluate whether to move forward. Pretend you are a dispassionate scientist hired to consider the odds of your next venture's success.

Over the years, I've worked with thousands of anxious students as they applied to colleges and graduate schools. Some would have rational concerns: "I don't think I'll get into Harvard." Most would have irrational concerns: "I don't think I'll get into Podunk State." With the latter concern, I asked students to step outside themselves and give some percentage chance of admission for a student with the same exact academic profile. Assuming the students made reasonable assessments, they would feel better.

Career issues are more complicated because there is no equivalent of *U.S. News & World Report* data for career outcomes. Nonetheless, if you engage in market analysis, you should be able to make reasonable predictions regarding potential success.

Roger was interested in law school, but news regarding unemployed attorneys worried him. Unquestionably, such news should be part of his evaluation of pursuing law school. Given Roger's high LSAT score and GPA, he was likely to gain admission to a top-twenty law school.

The dispassionate scientist would suggest that his data gathering be focused on employment for students from upper-echelon law schools. He discovered that the bulk of unemployed lawyers came from lower-tiered schools. From the perspective of a dispassionate scientist, he better understood his odds, and that propelled him to move forward.

Strategy: Dealing Effectively with Ambiguity is a Valuable Life Skill

Jack DeGioia, the revered long-time president of Georgetown University, was kind enough to provide guidance to me when I was in my twenties. One of his nuggets of wisdom was: "The ability to deal effectively with ambiguity is one of life's most underrated skills." He gave this counsel in relation to one of my career choice points: I had been offered a position as an assistant attorney general for the newly formed nation of Palau, a beautiful island in the South Pacific. Similar to the Marshall Islands, Palau had a protectorate relationship with the United States and thus sought out US government attorneys to help build their legal system. I was bored in my work prosecuting securities violations in Washington, DC, and I initially thought my wife and I could enjoy a couple of years in an idyllic paradise. I would be one of a small group of attorneys prosecuting crimes and representing the government in other high-level matters. Sounded great.

My excitement soon sunk into a morass of ambiguity. If I spent two years off the normal legal track would future employers think this move interesting or flaky (outcome ambiguity)? Palau did not have Internet access at the time, so applying for jobs back in the United States would be very complicated (process ambiguity). I was frozen in analysis paralysis. The decision was ultimately forged by personal considerations—my wife and I wanted to start a family and thought it best to have our first child near our extended family.

I was twenty-eight years old at the time and had not yet adequately developed the skills to deal with ambiguity. Through the decades that followed, I reflected on President DeGioia's advice many times. As a society, we tend not to think of psychological strengths as skills that can be developed, or that such skills have practical application. But neither is true. In *Siddhartha*, Herman Hesse's classic novel inspired by the life of the Buddha, Siddhartha explains one of his skills to a potential employer: "I can wait." Learning to be patient was a skill Siddhartha had cultivated and that proved highly valuable to the merchant who hired him. Similarly, the ability to deal with ambiguity is a skill that should be practiced. Learn to be OK with uncertainty. Not only will the ability to deal effectively with ambiguity decrease your anxiety levels, it will enable you to take calculated risks for career advancement.

"I Want It All."

"What do you want from your career?" is a common career-counseling question, and "I want it all," is a common response, particularly from idealists. You might be waiting for Mr. or Miss Right, or The Perfect Career, but this can only cause problems when searching for a spouse or a career. I often listen to desires that create an immediate sense of improbability:

"I want to earn a lot of money, and I don't want the job to be too demanding."

"I want to be my own boss, and I want security."

"I want to be a constant presence for my children, and I want to travel."

Strategy: Use the Must-Want Continuum to Prioritize

I'm not one to burst bubbles, but each career field has its bumps. To sort out which bumps matter, I make my clients evaluate their options through a "Must-Want Continuum." I created this paradigm after hearing clients list their desires without any prioritization and without recognizing that many of their desires conflicted with how things play out in the real world. Those highly paid/low-pressure jobs are not plentiful. Younger clients, in particular, will list their career demands then cross off possibilities if one of those demands is not met.

I make my clients place their career desires along a continuum with Must on one end and Want (as in nice to have but not essential) on the other end. Prioritization does wonders to burst magical thinking. Separating the essential from the added benefit, but not highly important, will help evaluate possibilities. If a client places high income far closer to Must than low pressure, then she can see what really matters to her. If your main goal is to maximize income, then you likely will be dealing with some pressure, and that's fine if low pressure provides only a small benefit. Similarly, those who tell me they want to have a full-time job, but want the freedom to work from home will need to categorize which is more important, as will those who want the autonomy of entrepreneurship and the relative security of organizational employment.

**Strategy: Understand That You Might Be Able
to Have It All, Just Not All at Once**

I also show clients that while it is possible to have it all, having it all at once is usually challenging. Jobs with world travel usually do not mix well with new mothers.

Intrapersonal Wisdom will propel you toward asking more refined questions in relation to having it all: "What am I willing to do to put myself in a position to have it all?" "What does 'have it all' mean to me?" and "What is most important to me right now?"

Fear Is the Foundational Block

Fear underlies all of the preceding psychological blocks, and it deserves its own section. What are you afraid of? Public failure? Lack of security? Being wrong? Disappointing yourself? Losing control? These psychological issues are often repressed but must be confronted.

Financial Failure

Our basic career fears involve money. If your current salary barely pays your bills, you have nothing saved, and are thousands of dollars in debt, it would be rational to fear quitting your job to start a business or enter a new field at a lower salary.

Some fears, however, are irrational or at least overstated. In response to questions about not moving forward with their dream careers, some clients respond: "I might starve or become homeless." Even if my clients are conveying only the figurative possibility that they may become unable to afford basic necessities, I tell them to stop being irrational.

My view emanates from a place of deep gratitude. We have extraordinary good fortune. If you lived during most every other historical era or in many places of the world today, both starvation and homelessness could become a reality if you were unable to earn money for an extended period of time.

As noted earlier, that you have the luxury of pondering career choice likely places you in fortunate enough circumstances that you have family, friends, and acquaintances who would help you if you were in dire straits, and multiple public and private safety nets that would further serve to buffer any fall. You will not starve, and it is highly unlikely that you will become homeless.[12]

Strategy: Separating the Rational from the Irrational
The first step to combat generalized fear is to separate rational from irrational fears. Confront the rational ones by evaluating the real downside and plan accordingly. As for the irrational fears, dealing with anxiety is complicated. I tell my clients who are angst ridden when contemplating career questions to role-play being a monk or a robot confronting similar issues. Strange, I know. But those who are advanced spiritually and those who are exclusively rational do not suffer anxiety. They simply deal with the challenges peacefully and rationally.

Your rational fear is financial instability, not starvation. Analytically evaluate how your career move would impact your finances if the venture failed: "If the business fails, we will have no savings left, my husband will have to work double shifts at the hospital, I'll have to work retail, and we'll have to rely on a home equity line of credit to get by until I get a job." With these facts in mind, you can make rational decisions about risk rather than grappling with imagined monsters under the bed.

---

12 I am not advocating recklessness based on the thought that you will be bailed out by your family or the government. Entrepreneurial Wisdom mandates careful evaluation of risk.

Public Failure

Are you afraid of failing in public? I understand that fear all too well. In my younger years, I worried what "they" would think. As I became more self-aware, I asked myself who "they" are and found that I did not know and did not really care.

I realized that if I failed, those who genuinely cared for me would still do so. People one step out of my circle of real friends and family were the "they," an undefined audience of people who were not really watching me. This part of "they" would barely give a moment's thought about my fortunes. Why? "They" are fully consumed with their own lives because of self-absorption and/or healthy attunement to what really matters to them. "They" don't care about my career or yours.

To illustrate this point, spend a few moments watching the audience the next time you attend any children's theatre or musical performance. Parents are singularly focused upon their own children, barely noticing anyone else's. The same concept holds true in relation to the career paths of others.

Strategy: Reevaluate How Much "They" Think about You

If you are not moving forward with a potentially great career plan because you fear negative public perception if you flounder, reevaluate your perception of how much others spend time thinking about you. If you think it will be embarrassing to lose your job or have your business fail because everyone will know and everyone will care, then you should realize that few will know and even fewer will care, at least in a negative way.

Those who do hear of your problems—and care about you—will wish you well and offer to help. Those who do not like you, or feel in competition with you, may have their moment of Schadenfreude, but you will never know. Moreover, you might seem more likeable to such envious types who are more likely to kick you when you are up then when you are down. And as anyone who has lived long enough to develop a modicum of wisdom knows, life is too short to worry about what those you don't respect think.

Personal Failure
You might be your toughest audience. Perfectionists have this issue. No one likes being wrong. But some people are overly self-critical, which makes being wrong particularly terrible for them. Taking a risk by definition means you might get it wrong. Your task is to treat yourself better if things don't go well.

Jessica had spent the last decade dreaming about opening a yoga studio. A meticulous planner, Jessica had the financing, location, teachers, and client base—she just had to take the leap. "But what if I do something wrong and it fails?" Jessica's practical downside was not too bad: she could go back to teaching at other yoga institutes, she was not too bothered by public perception, and her peer group and family were supportive.

But Jessica was her own toughest critic: "I'll beat myself up over everything that goes wrong." Even if the venture didn't fail, Jessica worried that she would constantly berate herself for the inevitable mistakes that come with starting a business.

"You'll be tough to work for." I said, knowing this was not true, as Jessica was very kindhearted.

"What do you mean?" Jessica asked.

"When your staff makes mistakes, you will be really tough on them."

"No, I'm not like that with others."

We then discussed what I already knew: Jessica treated others far better than she treated herself. She agreed that she treated others well not only because she wanted to be nice, but because doing so was also more effective. She then understood the point: being self-critical was not serving her.

Strategy: Apply the Golden Rule to Yourself

Are you worried about disappointing yourself? Learn to treat yourself as you would treat others. As children, most perfectionists created internal programming along the lines of "If I'm tough on myself, I will get it right." At some point, such criticism isn't necessary for success. On the contrary—you will stop yourself from moving forward for fear of your worst critic: **you**

Transactional vs. Opportunity Costs

As you venture into Exploratory and Pay-Your-Dues Work, you will have to grapple with understanding the balance between these costs.

Transactional Costs are all the time, money, energy, and psychological angst spent to move into a new field. Transactional costs block people from moving forward.

Time: Time is a major cost in two ways—it takes time to seek out and obtain new opportunities, and it takes months or years, not days, to make most successful career transitions.

Money: To move into a new field, you may need to take a cut in pay, or invest in further training or credentials.

Energy: Transitions demand increased energy and added willpower.

Psychological Angst: To move forward you will need to overcome the psychological blocks addressed earlier.

There are additional transactional costs for some people: you might need to move to a different location, or your career change may affect your relationships. Both are significant, but each is too uniquely personal to address generically here.

Opportunity Costs are all the time, money, energy, and psychological angst spent doing something other than what you want to be doing for your career. As the trite but true adage suggests, the best time to start a life-enhancing move was yesterday; the next best time is today. Simply put, you are incurring opportunity costs every day if you could be doing something better with your time.

What stops people from moving forward? Most everyone overestimates transactional cost and underestimates opportunity cost.

The All-Too-Common Tale of Opportunity Cost

Pete told me his career tale. He started in his current field twenty years ago when he was twenty-five years old. He didn't like the job on his first day and was convinced within the first few months that this career field wasn't a fit. The job was reasonably well paying and prestigious. His boss was fine, as were his coworkers and quality of life. So while he didn't like his actual work, the overall job wasn't horrible. He stayed on and did not engage in any meaningful Exploratory Work.

Twenty-five became thirty, and Pete's work life was more or less the same. Doing the same work made him feel both comfortable, since he knew how to do his job well, and bored, because he was not learning anything new. During this time, he got married and bought his first house.

Pete relayed that he never engaged in a transactional vs. opportunity cost analysis. His thoughts were: "I'm married and just bought a house. This is not the time to switch jobs." He did not think through the opportunity costs he was incurring.

Thirty became thirty-five, and Pete's work life became mildly worse: the semifun socialization with his twenty-something colleagues disappeared, and his new boss—while not an ogre—was a downgrade from his old boss.

Nonetheless, his first child came along and his wife went from working full time to part time. It was now a tough time to switch fields. When he reflected, Pete noted that his younger self focused only on the now higher transactional costs of switching jobs and gave little thought to opportunity costs.

Thirty-five became forty, and Pete's work life became worse—at least mentally—as he had been passed up for a couple of promotions and was now "old for his title." He noticed what I have preached: if you don't like what you do, eventually you won't be that good at it either. His colleagues who liked the work more than he did went the extra mile during projects, were more engaged during meetings, and were more willing stay late and come in on weekends. During this time, another child came along and Pete's wife gave up her career altogether. From a practical perspective, switching fields was now extremely tough. Indeed, the transactional costs were now so high it was understandable that he did not give much thought to what he was giving up.

Forty became forty-five, and The Great Recession transpired during these years. Given the economic squeeze on his company, management—as well as his latest boss—grew more demanding, and Pete's coworkers grew more competitive, paranoid, and stressed. His quality of life was now affected, as he had to work later and often on weekends. As always, he didn't really like his work activities.

Pete came to see me because his company told him they were going to lay him off. Pete pleaded for his job and ultimately agreed to a 30 percent cut in pay, along with the knowledge that his job would be perpetually on thin ice. He wondered how he wound up begging to keep a job he never liked.

When I met Pete, we discussed these realizations:

(1) Pete would have been fortunate if he had been forced to consider switching fields at a younger age. It is far better to have high-level misery early in a mismatched career. If Pete had had the same circumstances in his twenties as he does presently, he would be in a different career now.

(2) Despite the temptation to say "now isn't the time to explore other fields," he realized that now is always a better time than five years from now. Specifically, at forty-five years old with two kids approaching college age, on top of all the other trappings of suburban living, now is not a good practical time for Pete to start Exploratory and Pay-Your-Dues Work to switch fields. However, "now" will be even worse at fifty.

Analyzing Transactional vs. Opportunity Cost Time: Pete's story illustrates how easy it is to underestimate the opportunity cost of time. Transactional costs almost always grow as one gets older. Those with children, mortgages, and car loans can't move as easily as those who are untethered from such responsibilities. This is one reason young people should be more willing to make dramatic transitions: opportunity cost almost always outdistances transactional cost when long stretches of life are considered. The thirty-year-old has to weigh forty years of not liking work (opportunity cost) versus whatever challenges (transactional costs) would be incurred to switch fields to a better fit. In such cases, the transactional costs pale in comparison to the opportunity cost of staying in an unhappy career. On the other hand, a sixty-year-old in a similar situation would have to be quite the romantic to switch career paths as the opportunity cost would be comparably smaller.

Money: Financial transactional costs are far more decipherable than the financial opportunity costs of pursuing a new career. You could determine that graduate school costs fifty thousand dollars; your pay will be cut by twenty thousand dollars; and you will have to rely on fifteen thousand dollars in savings for the next six months. Those numbers are often literal transactional financial costs.

In comparison, opportunity cost related to money is far more nebulous. You might have data that leads to reasonable predictions about your new path's projected earnings, but ultimately you will have to take a leap of faith on your potential return on investment—sometimes a very big leap.

Short-Term Expense for Likely Long-Term Gain

If you are moving into a field that generally pays more than your current field, your financial analysis is relatively easy. David fretted over spending one hundred thousand dollars on an MBA. He concluded that completing that degree would likely increase his salary by twenty thousand to fifty thousand dollars per year over ten years. His rational brain embraced the decision. Nonetheless, he came to me because he couldn't move forward. "Likely" was the term that stopped him in his tracks. He wanted "definitely." After going through the analysis, I, too, concluded "likely." I forcefully explained, however, that his alternative was staying put, and in that case he would "likely" make less money. He hadn't thought of the issue that way. This reverse probability analysis led him to move forward.

Short-Term Expense for Uncertain Long-Term Gain

The financial potential of most career paths cannot be analyzed easily. Jane wondered if she should spend fifty thousand dollars for a degree in nonprofit management. Would Jane be guaranteed a higher-paying job after graduation? No. She was currently a midlevel account executive at a marketing firm. Some nonprofits pay very well, and she could potentially earn much more than her current salary. On the other hand, many nonprofits do not pay well.

Jane was talented and driven: she had "the stuff" to lead a substantial nonprofit. Still, upon graduation she might have to take a job that paid the same as or less than she earned now. So at least for a few years, the financial investment would not make sense. The hope, but not guarantee, would be that she would make more or at least as much money over time.

That's where envisioning happiness and success helps. Jane had been blocked because she was thinking exclusively from a success perspective. This analysis was entirely inconclusive. I pointed out that she was fairly certain she would remain unhappy in her current career field and was highly confident that pursuing a career in nonprofit management would lead to greater happiness. From a financial success perspective, her chances of greater success were fifty-fifty. But from a happiness perspective (meaning/purpose), the chances of greater happiness were very high. She smiled and moved forward.

Short-Term Expense for Long-Term...Who Knows?

There is always uncertainty for those who enter new careers. That does not compare to the uncertainty of starting new ventures. As any entrepreneur has experienced, the variables associated with starting a business make projections more art than science.

For years Clint had dreamed of starting his own company. He would get to the point of committing, and then step back. He went through this pattern repeatedly because of the financial unknown. When we met, he was hopeful I could predict how his business would perform.

Clint painstakingly went through his meticulous analysis. I couldn't make any better forecasts than Clint. We certainly discussed psychological angst and his need to deal with ambiguity. Those skills need some time to cultivate. Fortunately, I knew one strategy that works very well in the short term.

Strategy: The Downside Backup Plan

What would happen if Clint's business failed? Starvation? Homelessness? Destitution? These invisible demons impeded Clint's progress.

We worked on creating a backup plan if Clint's business did not succeed. Clint's wife also worked, and had encouraged him to "go for it" because he had become increasingly unhappy in his job and was bringing this unhappiness home. Although she did not have a high enough income to make all of their current bills, she could cover the mortgage, basic utilities, and basic groceries. He estimated that they would likely run a monthly three-thousand-dollar deficit with their current standard of living, but a monthly two-thousand-dollar deficit if they cut out luxuries like dining out, vacations, and pricey phone plans.

Could Clint get a part-time job? "Probably. My brother runs a UPS store. He is always looking for part-time workers." Clint would have to swallow his pride, but realized that if he were desperate, he likely could earn a thousand dollars a month working for his brother. He would still run a deficit until he figured out his next plan, but this seemed more manageable. Clint also had access to an eighty-thousand-dollar home equity line of credit. I'm mindful of suggesting that my clients rely on credit, but Clint needed to know that he was not going to starve anytime soon, even if his business failed.

Energy: Exploratory and Pay-Your-Dues Work take energy. I can hear the internal sighs when the thought of having to "work harder than I already am" enters one's mind. Thoughts of transactional energy costs make my clients weary: "While working full time, you want me to take night classes? Start a business on the side? Get a second job to save money for graduate school?"

Yes, yes, and yes! Entrepreneurial and Intrapersonal Wisdom require you to embrace work. Work requires energy. The good news is that the energy from your passion should push you onward. I remember looking at my calendar sometime during the first phase of starting The Learning Consultants: I had worked one hundred and seven days straight but was surprised because I wasn't tired, burned out, or stressed. As long as I stayed in balance—spent time with my family and friends, exercised, ate right, and slept enough—I could work every day because I loved my work. I still feel that way. And while now I regularly take long vacations and three-day weekends, it is only from the choice of wanting to spend more time affirmatively doing other things I love, like being with my family and travelling. If I had to work one hundred and seven days in a row again, I would be fine. Happy work creates its own energy.

In contrast, if you are in a job that you don't like, you will continually operate in a low, flat energy state. Your level of energy will decrease over time.

Psychological Angst: Ironically, every day you spend in a career that you don't like adds to the emotional difficulty of leaving. We are hardwired to desire security. Stable environments—even unhappy ones—are secure; unknown environments are scary. The reptilian part of your brain equates the rock you are under—your dreadful job—with security.

To overcome your biological programming, your rational brain will need to sort out the differences between real and perceived risk. For example, you are far more likely to get hurt approaching a deer—one kick and you are headed to the ER—than coming close to a nonvenomous snake. The real risk of approaching the cute deer outweighs the perceived risk of the scary snake.

There is little doubt that you will perceive risk in venturing off toward your passion—this perceived risk and the real risk might be reasonably aligned, and you might be correct in estimating the real risk of your venture. In my experience, however, it is far more likely that you will overestimate the perception of risk of moving to an appealing new career and greatly underestimate the real risk of staying in a mismatched career. More simply put, you probably won't regret taking a big career risk for a field you like, but you will definitely regret staying put in a field you hate.

The Real Risk of Staying In a Career You Don't Like
Are you in a job that you don't like, but don't want to leave because of the risk? Think again. We live in a ruthlessly competitive capitalist system. Those who don't like what they do will not push themselves to get better. During their off-hours, they'll avoid work. They will give unconscious signals indicating their unhappiness. Their boss and coworkers will pick up those sighs, subtle eye rolls, fake smiles, and all other indications of their wish to be anywhere else but at work.

Others will like your job or be driven enough to push themselves to succeed at your job. Soon enough, they will be better than you at what you do and will get promoted over you. New applicants will demonstrate enthusiasm for the job you disdain. At some point, someone else will take your job because if you are not happy in your career, you won't be successful either.

When I was a summer associate at a Washington, DC, law firm, I walked into the law library and spotted one of the partners reading a journal of recent legal decisions. He wasn't merely reading the headlines; he was digesting all fifty-plus pages of dense legalese. He sat in a large reading chair as if he were devouring a great novel. I was standing next to one of the partners, who noted: "Alex does this every month when new decisions come out in the legal journal." That's why Alex was successful.

I also recall Lisa, a paralegal at the same firm. While she was not overtly disrespectful, she looked perpetually bored and unhappy. When given assignments, she politely accepted but looked like she just added a fifty-pound weight to her cart. She was let go by the end of the summer.

Unhappy Work Leads to Unsuccessful Work

Consider a hypothetical scenario in which a new batch of workers with equal native abilities is divided into those who like and don't like their work. During off-hours, those who like their careers will think about how to improve. They will come in early and leave late. They won't mind putting in time on the weekends or other off-hours. While at work, they will be engaged, thus learning at a fast pace. Management will pick up on their positive body language, energy, and attitude. All of these factors will help them move upward.

Those who don't like their careers will do none of those things. After work, they won't think about work except the anxiety it causes. If they come in early, stay late, or work on weekends, it will stem from a boss's order or simply the worry about keeping their jobs. They will be bored at work and thus learn at a slow pace. Management will pick up on negative body language, the looks of disinterest, and those grumbles about working late.

You have to leave work you don't like, not only because you are unhappy, but because soon enough you won't be good at what you do. That is real risk.

Strategy for Evaluating Transactional vs. Opportunity Cost

When I suggest a new career path, I do an exercise with a client as soon as the protests about transactional costs commence. I head to our white board and precisely note all potential transactional costs. I then try to give a value in the amount of years of unhappiness/lack of success their transition may cost. We consider the Pay-Your-Dues and McDonald's Work required for the new field and give an estimated value in years for the amount of transactional cost required.

I contrast this with the estimated years of unhappiness/lack of success related to opportunity cost. Transactional cost often amounts to two to five years, whereas opportunity cost almost always amounts to decades.

If You Are Unhappy at Work, at Best You Will Be an Unhappy Success

I further push my clients by noting that if they stay in work they don't like, they will soon be caught in a greater trap—they will become unhappy successes.

Each year you stay in your field should lead to greater tangible benefits. These success gold stars will feel good in the short term but will gradually become handcuffs. Your wrists will feel tighter with each raise and promotion. From an emotional perspective, you will find it more difficult to go backward in terms of income and position even if you truly believe the new path you are considering would lead to happiness. At some point, it will not make practical—as opposed to emotional—sense for you to quit a job that you hate. When you compare your now-elevated income, position, and expertise with whatever position you are comparing in a new field, you will be faced with an increasingly disproportionate reason to stay.

So if you are unhappy at work, you will either be unhappy and unsuccessful, or, at best, an unhappy success.

Situational Analysis: The First Concrete Step

Turning ideas into reality is the essence of entrepreneurship. Plenty of people are idea generators. Idealists are particularly adept at creating dreamlike possibilities. Making ideas a reality separates the dreamers from the doers, but this section is not about the execution of ideas. How to get things done has been covered quite extensively by a cottage industry of productivity experts.[13] Instead, we will cover situational analysis—the first step in taking a career idea and making it into a career reality.

Many of my clients have good ideas regarding what they want to do but stop before they start because they do not evaluate how the idea will work in the real world. Situational analysis will save you time, energy, and expense by separating plausible ideas from crazy ones.

Since I am an entrepreneur and a career counselor, I hear a large number of business ideas. The ideas are not necessarily bad, but most people do not carefully analyze how to make them reality. Ethan had developed an app idea regarding biofeedback monitors to help employers monitor worker engagement. It was an intriguing concept.

---

13 *Getting Things Done*, by David Allen, seems to be the most recent seminal work on the subject. My original favorite was *The 7 Habits of Highly Effective People*, by the late, great Stephen Covey.

To develop the technology, he likely needed several million dollars in venture capital, and he came for help in seeking such investment. But he hadn't thought about the likely legal hurdles involved in hooking up anyone to such devices, or about the challenges of selling to thousands of individual companies. No investor will touch his idea unless those challenges are overcome.

Before committing to action, successful entrepreneurs analyze their work and life situations to determine the likely challenges, risks, and opportunities of a specific path. Entrepreneurs—at least the good ones—are usually not extreme risk takers. While they may have a higher risk tolerance for pulling the trigger, they are not gunslingers. They weigh the odds and assess the pros and cons, thus their willingness to move forward stems from confidence in their situational analysis. Entrepreneurs evaluate questions such as:

Is the entrepreneurial opportunity a good calculated risk?

Do I have the resources/skills to make the venture work?

Does my life situation enable me to devote sufficient energy to the endeavor?

You can analyze potential career choices with a similar set of questions. Idealists often avoid mundane topics, but to ensure the "successful" part of the Path of Abundance you must deal with the nitty-gritty of the real world.

The Complexity of Situational Analysis

The complexity of analyzing each individual's life/work situation is among the key reasons computer software cannot provide precise career path answers. Sal came to me after he had undergone an extensive and expensive series of career tests. Investment banking and other high-finance jobs were highest on the list of matched career paths. I reviewed the questions asked, as well as his answers. Making a great deal of money was far and away his number one job value. He was also interested in the financial markets and had a high math aptitude. It made sense that high-finance jobs were recommended.

Nonetheless, situational analysis made pursuing such jobs highly unlikely. Sal was part of a very tight-knit family that lived far away from New York and other metropolitan areas where investment banking opportunities existed. He wanted to remain close to his family and continue living in a rural part of the country. Furthermore, he graduated college from a local state school. Prestige-obsessed investment banks were not going to review his resume without high-level personal connections to get him in the door.

So how would someone with strong situational-analysis skills handle the situation? Knowing that making a lot of money was his major success goal, and staying close to his family was his major happiness goal, Sal could focus on jobs or businesses in his geographic area with the potential to make a lot of money. Or he might knowingly try to buck the odds and start a job in high finance despite living in an area not traditionally suited for such work, just as Warren Buffet did in Omaha, Nebraska.

So, if you have an idea for what you want to do, that's wonderful. Now it's time to engage in real-world situational analysis.

Conclusion

Our current career challenges present a psychological paradox: we should be profoundly grateful for what we have in our current world (state of contentment) yet we should strive to reach our human potential (state of ambition).

I started the book by citing the need for gratitude. From an objective perspective, most every career in the knowledge economy is better than most every other career over the vast expanse of human history. Cubicle nation is still preferable to twelve hours tending crops or laying brick in the hot sun.

Nonetheless, we are in a work revolution that will leave the majority of workers struggling or worse. Unlike in the twentieth century, where early commitment to a career track and a willingness to trade variety for stability was the norm, the New World of Work requires the ability to deal with continual turbulence. Constant change is exciting and unnerving. Those with Intrapersonal and Entrepreneurial Wisdom will be best positioned to chart and adjust their course to find work that leads to happiness and success.

Clarifying what happiness and success mean to you will be part of your inner work, as will learning to navigate the various psychological blocks that stymie many people from bravely moving through fear toward what they really want.

Understanding the "why" of your work will provide the meaning necessary to move through the tough parts of career development. Knowing the reason for your

McDonald's Work and your Pay-Your-Dues Work will provide the determination to get you through your day.

What should you do after you put this book down? Commit to Exploratory Work. It is the work that you are doing right now as your eyes meet the page. It is the work that most people don't do, so you are already ahead of the pack. Our website, Career Path of Abundance, www.careerpathofabundance.com, has plenty of free resources. In addition, I'm always happy to hear from readers. Feel free to contact me directly. If I can help you formally or informally, I'll be glad to do so.

Developing key insights about your personality preferences, core motivations, and values through reading, reflecting, and using personality-profiling tools will go a long way toward building your Intrapersonal Wisdom. Engaging in rigorous situational analysis to evaluate potential career options will help build your Entrepreneurial Wisdom.

We are very lucky. We should acknowledge our delightful good fortune. Still, part of our luck includes having the capacity to pursue careers that suit us. As such, we have the responsibility to make the most of our good timing to be alive during this exciting transformational period. You don't want to wonder on your death bed why you settled for unhappy and/or unsuccessful work, particularly when you had the opportunity for so much more. Your life is time, and your career takes up a lot of time. Opportunity cost is a silent killer.

If you are in a job you don't like, remember that you chose to accept the job regardless of the circumstances that may have led you there. Given that you have choice, you—and you alone—have the responsibility to figure out your Path of Abundance. Try to have fun doing so. Approach the process with as much optimism as possible.

You will develop Intrapersonal and Entrepreneurial Wisdom. You will create a happy and successful career. Go.

BIBLIOGRAPHY

Allen, David. *Getting Things Done: The Art of Stress-Free Productivity.* New York: Penguin, 2015.

Bolles, Richard Nelson. *What Color Is Your Parachute?: A Practical Manual for Job-hunters & Career-changers.* Berkeley: Ten Speed, 1995.

Capuano, Daryl. *Motivate Your Son: Inspire Your Boy to Be Engaged in School, Excited for College, and Energized for Success.* Old Saybrook, CT: The Learning Consultants, 2012.

Covey, Stephen R. *The 7 Habits of Highly Effective People: Restoring the Character Ethic.* New York: Simon & Schuster, 1989.

Csikszentmihalyi, Mihaly. *Flow: The Psychology of Optimal Experience.* New York: Harper & Row, 1990.

Ferriss, Timothy. *The 4-hour Work Week: Escape 9-5, Live Anywhere, and Join the New Rich.* Chatham, UK: Vermilion, 2011

Frankl, Viktor Emil, and Ilse Lasch. *Man's Search for Meaning; an Introduction to Logotherapy. A Newly Revised and Enlarged Edition of "From Death-camp to Existentialism,"* New York: Simon & Schuster, 1970.

Friedman, Thomas L. *The World Is Flat: A Brief History of the Twenty-first Century.* New York: Farrar, Straus & Giroux, 2005.

Gladwell, Malcolm. *Blink: The Power of Thinking without Thinking*. New York: Little, Brown, 2005.

Gladwell, Malcolm. *Outliers: The Story of Success*. London: Penguin, 2009.

Guillebeau, Chris. *The $100 Startup: Reinvent the Way You Make a Living, Do What You Love, and Create a New Future*. New York: Crown Business, 2012.

Handy, Charles B. *The Age of Unreason*. Boston: Harvard Business School, 1989.

Hesse, Hermann. *Siddhartha*. New York: New Directions, 1951.

Pink, Daniel H. *Free Agent Nation: How America's New Independent Workers Are Transforming the Way We Live*. New York: Warner, 2001.

Roose, Kevin. *Young Money: Inside the Hidden World of Wall Street's Post-Crash Recruits*. New York: Grand Central, 2014. Kindle edition.

Salinger, J. D. *The Catcher in the Rye*. New York: Bantam, 1966.

Schwartz, Barry. *The Paradox of Choice: Why More Is Less*. New York: Ecco, 2004.

Sinetar, Marsha. *Do What You Love, The Money Will Follow: Discovering Your Right Livelihood*. New York: Dell, 1989.

Note

In order to ensure the confidentiality of clients, all identifying details related to clients and their case histories have been altered. This includes names, professions, and any story elements that could lead to identification.

Acknowledgments

The biggest thank you is for my father, Len Capuano. His complete integrity, selflessness, and overall strong character educated me on how to live far more than all my years of schooling. Moreover, all my opportunities in life originated due to his work ethic. Everything I have done stems from standing on his shoulders.

In relation to the creation of this book, there are a few that deserve special thanks, listed here alphabetically:

Attilio Albani, a master craftsman in the business world, for sharing his abundant Entrepreneurial Wisdom;

Paul Borgese for showing me the brilliant promise of the New World of Work so many years ago;

Jesse Brockwell for his outstanding contributions to The Learning Consultants;

Rob and Jean Card for uniquely blending the best aspects of life and work friendship;

Cheryl Jacobs for answering all my questions when I was a young attorney, and for continuing to share her wisdom about life to this day;

Sue Jacobs Matzen for going far above and beyond in my own career transition and for demonstrating the potential for creating extraordinary career success anywhere in the world;

and

John and Mary Penny for so expertly raising Francie, being the best in-laws ever, and demonstrating the most important wisdom of all - familial wisdom.

About the Author

Daryl Capuano is the CEO of The Learning Consultants, www.learningconsultantsgroup.com, Connecticut's largest private education consultancy, and the lead career counselor for its career development subsidiaries Career Path of Abundance, www.careerpathofabundance.com and Career Counseling Connecticut, www.careercounselingconnecticut.com. Recently named to *Who's Who in America,* Daryl is a nationally known education expert and is the author of the 2012 book *Motivate Your Son,* as well as numerous magazine articles on educational issues. Daryl is a featured speaker on career and educational issues on a local and national level.

Daryl lives in Old Saybrook, CT, with his wife and three children, and can be reached at (860) 510-0410 or via e-mail at dcapuano@LearningConsultantsGroup.com.